Transcendent Wisdom

by Tenzin Gyatso
The Dalai Lama of Tibet

A Teaching on the Wisdom Section of Shantideva's
Guide to the Bodhisattva Way of Life.

Translated, edited and annotated by B. Alan Wallace

Snow Lion Publications
Ithaca, New York

Snow Lion Publications
P.O. Box 6483
Ithaca, New York 14851
USA

Printed in the USA

ISBN 1-55939-030-1

Library of Congress Cataloging-in-Publication Data

Bstan-'dzin-rgya-mtsho, Dalai Lama XIV, 1935–
    Transcendent wisdom / Tenzin Gyatso, the Dalai Lama of Tibet ; the
wisdom section of Shantideva's guide to the Bodhisattva way of life,
translated and annotated by B. Alan Wallace.
        p.   cm.
    Includes bibliographical references.
    ISBN 1-55939-030-1
    1. Śantideva, 7th cent.   Bodhicaryāvatāra.   Chapter 9.
    2. Mahayana Buddhism—Doctrines.   I. Wallace, B. Alan.
BQ3147.B78   1994
294.3'42—dc20
                                                        94-7562
                                                        CIP

Table of Contents

Foreword

This work consists of a translation from the Sanskrit of the ninth chapter of a work entitled *A Guide to the Bodhisattva Way of Life*[1] by the Indian scholar and contemplative Shantideva.[2] This chapter, named "Transcendent Wisdom," sets forth the Centrist, or Madhyamika view of Buddhist philosophy in the context of other Buddhist and non-Buddhist views. From a Western perspective it is philosophical in content; yet it has a definite religious tone to it, and it also belongs to a contemplative discipline that presents empirical means for testing its conclusions.

The translation of this text has been made primarily on the basis of a commentary in classical Tibetan by the 14th-century Tibetan master Tsongkhapa.[3] However, reference has also been made to the Sanskrit commentary by Prajñākaramati[4] and to another Tibetan commentary by a major student of Tsongkhapa.[5] The text is accompanied by a translation from spoken Tibetan of an oral commentary presented by H.H. the Dalai Lama, Tenzin Gyatso, during the summer of 1979 in Rikon, Switzerland.[6] This commentary was delivered before an assembly of roughly a thousand Tibetans and a few score Westerners, and it clearly assumes some background in Buddhist philosophy on the part of the listeners. The "Transcendent Wisdom'' chapter of Shantideva's classic treatise is known among Buddhist scholars as a challenging and profound exposition of the pinnacle of Buddhist philosophy. Hopefully this translation will further elucidate this text for those seeking an understanding of the Buddhist Centrist view and its relevance to contemporary thought.

ACKNOWLEDGEMENTS

This translation was completed during my years of study at Amherst College, culminating in December, 1986. I am particularly grateful to Robert Thurman, then Professor of Religion at Amherst College for his careful reading of the text and commentary. I would also like to thank Vesna Acimovic for her corrections of the Sanskrit translation.

While making the initial translation of the Sanskrit text, I used the version edited by P.L. Vaidya (Buddhist Sanskrit Text Series). I also consulted the Tibetan translation published by the Tibetan Cultural Printing Press in Dharamsala, India, and Stephen Batchelor's English translation of the text. While working on later drafts, I consulted Michael Sweet's translation in his 1977 doctoral dissertation in Buddhist Studies at the University of Wisconsin, entitled *Śāntideva and the Mādhyamika: The Prajñāpāramitā-Pariccheda of the Bodhicāryāvatāra.*

The Wisdom Section of Shantideva's
Guide to the Bodhiattva Way of Life
with a commentary by H.H. the Dalai Lama,
Tenzin Gyatso

H.H. the Dalai Lama

The Place of Wisdom
in Spiritual Practice

1. This entire preparation the Sage taught for the sake
   of wisdom. Thus, one wishing to bring an end to
   suffering should develop wisdom.

"This entire preparation" refers to the first five transcendent practices of generosity and so on;[1] or it may refer to meditative absorption.[2] All of these were taught by Buddha Shakyamuni in order to cultivate ultimate wisdom. In order for the realization of emptiness to arise in the mind, it is not necessary for one to engage in the other transcendent practices as well. According to the view of the author of this text and of Chandrakirti and Buddhapalita, Listeners[3] and Solitary Sages[4] overcome spiritual hindrances on their respective Paths of Seeing and of Meditation by means of the view of emptiness.[5] Thus, the practice of transcendent generosity and so on is not necessary for the cultivation of that view; nor is it necessary for eliminating the afflictive obscurations.[6]

What is the nature of wisdom? The view of emptiness entailing the integration of meditative quiescence[7] and insight[8] acts as the antidote for cognitive obscurations;[9] and with that view one experiences the subtle mode of existence of entities.[10] It is a wisdom that arises from meditation. But such wisdom alone is insufficient for overcoming those obscurations. Without being combined with a great store of virtue, that wisdom cannot be an antidote for the cognitive obscurations.[11] The major obstacles to the attainment of full spiritual awakening are the cognitive obscurations. Ultimate wisdom is their direct antidote. To cultivate that, this series of practices must be followed, thereby accumulating great virtue. Thus it is said: "This entire preparation the Sage taught for the sake of wisdom." Thus, one who wishes to bring an end to the suffering of oneself and others should develop such wisdom.

There are no teachings of the Buddha that are not means for living creatures to attain prosperity[12] and true felicity.[13] True felicity refers to liberation and omniscience, and to attain either, the view of emptiness is necessary. To dispel either the afflictive obscurations or the cognitive obscurations one must cultivate the view of emptiness. Thus, the entire "method" element of the Buddha's teachings, not only transcendent generosity and so on, was given for the sake of cultivating wisdom. The Listeners and Solitary Sages must also develop wisdom with the aid of the method element; wisdom cannot be gained without it. Here the term "method" does not refer to the spirit of awakening[14] or to taking upon oneself the responsibility for the welfare of others. There are many virtues such as concentration that are cultivated with the motivation of aspiring to gain one's own release from the cycle of rebirth.[15] In this way, by following the Three Trainings,[16] mental afflictions[17] are eliminated. All those methods were taught for the sake of liberation.

Part One:
The Methods Needed for Cultivating Wisdom

1 Introduction to the Two Truths that Comprise Reality

THE CLASSIFICATION OF THE TWO TRUTHS

> 2. The twofold truth is considered to be conventional and ultimate. [Ultimate] reality is not an object of the intellect; the intellect is called "conventional."

There are many types of wisdom relating to the plurality of phenomena[1] and the fundamental nature of reality. We are concerned now with the supreme wisdom that acts as the antidote for the fundamental cause of the cycle of existence[2]—namely, grasping onto true existence—and the instincts[3] for such grasping, which are cognitive obscurations. Such wisdom is the view by which one realizes emptiness; one thereby knows the fundamental nature of reality.

We need to understand the essential nature of the broad diversity of phenomena. For example, if we are obliged to be involved frequently with a man who exhibits a personality that is true only on the surface, as well as another basic personality, it is important for us to know both of them. To engage in a relationship with this person that does not go awry, we must know both aspects of his personality. To know only the facade that he presents is insufficient; we need to know his basic disposition and abilities. Then we can know what to expect from him; and he will not deceive us.

Likewise, the manifold events in the world are not non-existent; they do exist. They are able to help and hurt us—no further criterion for existence is necessary. If we do not understand their fundamental mode of existence, we are liable to be deceived, just as in the case of being involved with a person whose basic personality we do not know.

Now phenomena existing as dependently related events[4] are those that change in dependence upon circumstances and those that appear in various ways due to circumstances. All of the preceding teachings concern phenomena subject to change. They change due to their dependence upon other events.[5] If events existed independently, they could not change. Since they are dependent, they lack an independent nature. Thus, when something appears either good or bad, it seems to have that as an essential trait; but if we inspect matters more closely, we see that it is fundamentally subject to change. Thus, entities have two natures, one essential and the other superficial.

The physical world around us is impermanent, and individual entities have their own specific natures. Because the events that make up this world are dependent upon conditions, they lack an independent self-nature. That absence of an independent self-nature is the essential mode of existence of entities. Since events have two modes of existence—superficial and essential—there exist two types of cognition: one ascertaining the former nature and the other, the latter nature.

What is the essential mode of existence?: lack of independence, and lack of existence from the object's own side. The absence of intrinsic being is the ultimate mode of existence of an entity. The mind that apprehends that ultimate nature, which appears in accordance with its reality, cognizes reality as it is. It is thus called "ontological understanding."[6] That reality is empty because it is devoid of the mode of existence that is to be refuted; and for that very reason, it is called "emptiness." There is no higher truth to be seen. The mind that sees that reality experiences truth as it is. Thus it is called "ultimate truth," the essential mode of existence. For all other truths, their mode of appearance and their essential mode of existence are incongruent. Thus, they are called deceptive and superficial.

Now for a single entity we must understand two modes of existence. That entity, which is capable of benefiting or harming, has both modes of existence. We should not think of the fundamental nature of existence being found elsewhere. Its own essential nature is its ultimate mode of existence. Both a superficial and ultimate nature are to be found in a single entity, and those are the Two Truths.

The mind that ascertains the essential nature of an object is an intelligence that investigates the ultimate. The other mind is conventional intelligence, superficial cognition. When the text speaks of the need of developing wisdom, it refers to the former type of intelligence. In order to realize ultimate truth, one needs to distinguish between ultimate and superficial truths.

The text speaks of two objects of knowledge: conventional and ultimate truth. Both are to be known. Ultimate truth is not directly ascertainable by a dualistic awareness. When one directly apprehends the ultimate nature of an entity, dualistic appearances vanish. Thus, the ultimate transcends dualistic awareness. Dualistic awareness is polluted by ignorance, so that the ultimate cannot appear to it.

It would be absurd to say that the ultimate is not ascertained by any type of awareness at all. When the text says "Reality is not an object of the intellect," that intellect refers to dualistic awareness only. The first phrase—"Reality is not an object of the intellect"—entails a defining characteristic of ultimate truth; and the second—"the intellect is called 'conventional' "—entails a defining characteristic of conventional truth. The objects of dualistic awareness are conventional truths.

PEOPLE WHO ASCERTAIN THE TWO TRUTHS

3. Two types of people are found: the contemplative and
   the common person. The [view of the] contemplative
   person invalidates [that of] the common person.

There are two types of individuals—contemplatives and common people—i.e. those who engage in philosophical investigation and those who do not. Moreover, among the former there
are higher and lower levels of investigation. Those who assert
phenomenal identitylessness are on a higher lever; and those
who deny it are on a lower level. Among the former are the
Idealists,[7] who advocate intrinsic reality, and above all are the
Centrists.[8]

Referring to those common people who do not engage in
philosophical investigation, the text says that their way of seeing
and describing the world [involving, for example, belief in a
personal identity] is invalidated by the experience of those who
do engage in such investigation. Likewise, the experience of
those engaged in higher investigations invalidates that of people on a more simplistic level.

4. Even [the views of] contemplatives are invalidated by
   [those of] successively higher [contemplatives], due to
   the difference of insight, [which they can acknowledge]
   in terms of a commonly accepted analogy. [Whatever
   their views, they strive in virtuous acts] for the sake
   of spiritual growth, [leaving conventional reality] im-
   mune to their analysis.

As mentioned previously, the views even of contemplatives
are invalidated by those of other contemplatives at higher levels
of investigation. These views are invalidated by reasoning. Even
among the Centrists there are two classes: Svatantrika [Indepen-
dents] and Prasangika [Critics]. And among the Prasangikas
there are different levels of contemplative insight even given
the same set of postulates. For a single reality of emptiness

there are different ways of experiencing it: an experience that is veiled with a general idea[9] and one that is not [e.g. on the Path of Seeing]. There are also distinctions in terms of the obscurations that successive insights are able to dispel. In each case the higher surmounts the lower.

If more simplistic views are logically annulled by higher ones, in order to recognize the refutation of one's own view, there must be a common basis of disputation. Here the author speaks of analogies that are accepted both by contemplatives and common people. For instance, dreams and hallucinations: When people in general remark that a certain experience was like a dream, that means that it did indeed occur, but they doubt whether it was real or true.[10]

If as a result of scrutiny, different modes of existence are distinguished, does this mean that such spiritual activities as selfless giving are pointless? No, such methods of spiritual practice are to be adopted for the sake of spiritual growth, without examination or scrutiny.[11] Whatever appears to people is to be accepted conventionally and one practices on that basis.[12]

5. Events are seen and also thought to be real by [common] people, and are not regarded as illusion-like. Here is the disagreement between the contemplative and the common person.

If contemplatives and common people are able to agree on a common basis of disputation, about what do they disagree? When spiritual teachings are given, there are bound to be different interpretations on many levels according to the subtlety and depth of insight of the listeners. For example, Realists assert the true existence of the body and mind; whereas Centrists assert them as lacking true existence: Even though they appear as true, they do not so exist, but are like illusions. Thus, on the basis of one teaching, different interpretations are made. In this way disagreement arises between contemplatives and common people.

QUALMS CONCERNING THE LACK OF INTRINSIC EXISTENCE

6. Form and so on, although perceived, are [established]
   by consensus; [their true existence] is not verifiably
   congized. Like the consensus that the impure and so
   on are pure and so forth, [such cognition] is false.

Qualm: If it is an error to think of form and so forth as real,
how can it be that we verifiably perceive them? What further
criterion beyond verifying perception is needed to establish the
true existence of entities?

Response: Such entities are indeed verifiably perceived. However, when we say "verifying cognition",[13] this suggests infal-
libility. It is a non-deceptive awareness with reference to the
appearance of a self-defining object.[14] Realists—those who assert true existence—have just this in mind when speaking of
verifying cognition. They believe that phenomena appear just
as they exist, and they appear to be truly existent. They call
a cognition that is non-deceptive with regard to that appearance "verifying."

Now in this [Centrist] context, infallible cognition is acknowledged, while denying that there is any such thing as even
conventional intrinsic existence. Such cognition is said to be
deceptive with regard to the *appearance* of phenomena as intrinsically existent. The Prasangikas, who hold this view, do
not accept verifying cognition with respect to such appearance.
Thus, they allow that a deceptive awareness may nevertheless
verify its object. Therefore, phenomena exist by the power of
consensus, not by their own intrinsic reality.[15]

Such phenomena as form are regarded as misleading, for
their mode of appearance and their mode of existence are not
in accord with each other. Common people regard impure objects as pure, for the way those objects appear belies the way
they actually exist.[16] Although they are thought by consensus
to be pure, that conviction is false. Likewise, although
phenomena are not truly existent, they appear as if they were;

and thus they are asserted to be misleading.[17]

7. In order for common people to enter [gradually into an experience of ultimate reality], [real] entities were indicated by the Lord. One may object that if ultimately they are not momentary, that is contrary to conventional reality.

Qualm: The Lord Buddha is recorded in the scriptures as saying that all composites are impermanent and all tainted things[18] are unsatisfactory. Thus, when the Buddha taught the Four Noble Truths, he spoke of sixteen attributes, including impermanence.[19] Are those not ultimate truths; are they not absolute?

Response: The Buddha taught these in order for people to enter into the experience of emptiness; but ultimately speaking, there is no such thing as the impermanence of a pot. Ultimately, events are not momentary. Ultimately, the object itself does not exist, so it has no properties such as impermanence.

Qualm: If one takes that position—that ultimately, events are not of a momentary nature—does that mean that the conventional presentation of phenomena as passing away moment by moment is incorrect?

8. There is no mistake, for [the wise, looking] upon the world see reality with the discernment of a contemplative. Otherwise, the conclusion that the female [body] is impure would be invalidated by common people.

Response: No, that is not incorrect. That momentary nature is established by conventionally verifying cognition, so we accept that on a conventional basis. All the sixteen attributes of the Four Noble Truths are conventionally realized by contemplatives, so we can accept them.

Qualm: Well then, can we not call those sixteen "reality"?

Response: Common people mistake things that are essentially impermanent as permanent, and impure things as pure. In comparison to such attitudes, the contemplative experiences reality.[20] It is conventional reality.

Qualm: Since common people and contemplatives have two different ways of seeing things, might not the contemplatives' conclusions be invalidated by those of common people?

Response: No. There is the distinction that the former are backed by verifiable knowledge.[21] Otherwise, if the contemplatives' views could be repudiated simply by general consensus, then the conclusion that the female body is impure would be invalidated, since ordinary people think of it as pure and attractive.[22]

9. In [your] reality [real merit is accrued from revering a real Buddha]; likewise, [we assert that illusion-like] merit [is accrued] from [revering] an illusion-like Victor. If sentient beings are like illusions, having died, how can they take birth again?

Qualm: If you deny true existence, do you still assert that one accumulates merit by making offerings to Awakened Beings and so on?

Response: Yes. One engages in illusion-like actions, and illusion-like fruits of those actions ensue. For example, Realists, who assert true existence, maintain that from real actions, real merit is accumulated and real results are experienced. The Centrists acknowledge the accumulation of merit and the effects of actions—but as not truly existent.

Qualm: If sentient beings are like illusions, how can they take birth again after having died?

10. As long as the complex of conditions [persists], so long even illusion functions. Why should a sentient being exist [more] truly [than an illusion] by the mere fact of its extended duration?

Response: An illusion is not truly existent. If an illusion appears as a horse or elephant, it does not exist as such. Although it is not real, it appears due to a complex of conditions, and it vanishes due to the cessation of that complex of conditions. So even an illusion depends upon causes and conditions. One cannot establish duration as a criterion for true existence.

11. There is no evil in such acts as the slaying of an illusory person, for [such an entity] has no mind; but in the case of one endowed with an illusory mind, evil and merit are produced.

Qualm: Although sentient beings are like illusions, killing is evil. Is it also the case that killing illusory beings is evil?
Response: Since the being who is "killed" has no mind, no evil occurs.[23] But illusion-like beings have illusion-like minds, so helping or harming them results in merit or evil respectively.

12. An illusory mind is not [originally] produced, for incantations and so forth lack such a capability. Diverse conditions produce, moreover, a variety of illusions. Nowhere is there a single condition that has the ability [to produce] everything.

Mind is something that must arise from a source similar to itself, as will be explained later on.[24] There is no way that an incantation can freshly create a mind. So in an illusion there is no creation of an illusory mind. One may create illusory horses and elephants but not an illusory mind.

From diverse conditions, a variety of illusions arise. Even though they are not real, they are produced by various conditions. A single condition cannot produce everything.

13. If it were the case that while being ultimately emancipated, one were [still] to be conventionally subject to rebirth, then a Buddha would also be subject to rebirth. In that case, what would be the point of the Bodhisattva way of life?

In treatises such as Nagarjuna's *Sixty Stanzas of Reasoning* there is reference to ultimate truth, the absence of intrinsic existence, as emancipation. The cycle of existence is conventional. There are three types of emancipation: natural, residual and non-residual.[26] The first of those is the mere absence of intrinsic existence. Thus, a single individual could abide simultaneously in the world and in emancipation. In reference to this, there is the question as to whether a Buddha is in the cycle of existence.[27]

14. If the conditions are not discontinued, even illusions
    do not cease. But due to the cessation of conditions,
    the conventional, too, does not occur.

Even illusions are dependent upon conducive conditions. If those conditions are not interrupted, neither are the ensuing illusions; and if the former cease, so do the latter. Thus, as long as the necessary conditions prevail, the cycle of existence, which is like an illusion, persists.[28] If those conditions cease, not only is there the natural emancipation of ultimate truth, even the conventional, momentary [i.e. rising and passing with each moment] continuum of the cycle of existence is cut. And that cessation is called emancipation.

For example, just as clouds vanish into an empty sky, so are the obscurations extinguished in the sphere of reality.[29] In that way the afflictive obscurations are dispelled by the influence of conditions, and thus they are eliminated even conventionally. That is called liberation.

2 *Critique of the Idealist View*

15. If even deceptive [cognition] does not exist, by what
    is illusion ascertained?

Since the Centrists deny the true existence of all entities,
then the awareness of illusion-like forms and so forth must
be devoid of an intrinsic identity. So, when an Idealist hears
that something lacks an intrinsic nature, he [or she] concludes
that it is utterly non-existent. And thus he [or she] asks: If
even the cognition of an illusion does not exist, by what is the
illusion known? The implication is that it would be ascertained
by nothing at all. To this the Centrist replies:

16. If for you illusion itself does not exist, then what is
    to be ascertained? You may respond that in reality it
    exists otherwise, simply as an expression of the mind.

Idealist: External objects do not exist. All possible entities
are of the nature of the subjective mind. They are substances
of the mind, lacking any other substance. We Idealists take
as our scriptural source the statement that the three realms
of existence[1] are of the nature of the mind.

Centrist: According to you, if entities existed externally, as they appear to, they would not be illusory. If they do not exist externally, despite appearances, they would be devoid of an intrinsic nature; and in your view that would make them utterly non-existent. In that case, if the illusion itself does not exist, then there would be nothing to ascertain.

Idealist: In reality an entity does not exist externally, as it appears. Phenomena, such as form, exist otherwise—as substances of the mind that apprehends them. Thus, they do not exist as external objects, nor are they utterly non-existent.

17. If the mind itself is an illusion, then what is seen by
    what? For the Protector of the World has said that the
    mind does not perceive the mind. Just as the blade
    of a sword cannot cut itself, so is it with the mind.

Centrist: You Idealists maintain that the mind is of the same nature as the object that it apprehends. If the subject and object are identical, how can anything be seen by anything? The scriptures also refute the possibility of something apprehending itself. In the *Crown Jewel Discourse*[2] the Buddha states that the mind does not perceive itself. The mind cannot see itself just as a blade cannot cut itself.

18. You may reply: It is like a lamp illuminating itself.
    A lamp does not illuminate [itself], since darkness does
    not conceal [itself].

Idealist: Just as a lamp illuminates the surrounding darkness, so does it illuminate itself. There may be the tacit assumption that if it cannot illuminate itself, it could not illuminate anything else. Likewise, just as awareness perceives other objects, so does it perceive itself.

Centrist: It is conventionally inappropriate to say that a lamp illuminates itself. Why? Because a lamp does not have the quality of darkness. If darkness is present, it can be dispelled, but since this is absent in a lamp, it is meaningless to speak of a lamp illuminating itself. This point is discussed at length in Nagarjuna's *Fundamental Wisdom*.[3]

19. A blue [thing] does not require another [blue thing]
for its blueness, as does a clear crystal. So the mind
is seen sometimes to depend on another, sometimes
not.

Idealist: For example, if one were to place a clear crystal on
a blue base, its blue appearance would be dependent upon some
other blue substance. Now something like a lapis luzuli gem
is blue from the very time it is created, so its blueness does
not depend upon another blue substance. Thus, just as there
are the two cases of dependence and lack of dependence on
another object, so are some cognitions dependent upon objects such as form, while others are focussed inward and perceive awareness only.

Centrist: To determine whether forms and so on exist, it is
indispensable to have a verifying cognition: If something can
be apprehended by a verifying cognition, it exists; if it cannot, it does not exist. In fact "something that can be ascertained by a verifying cognition" is the definition of something
having a basis in reality.[4] All [Buddhist schools] agree on this
point.

Therefore, if there is no verifying cognition to establish the
existence of something, one cannot claim that it exists. When
one claims that there is verifying cognition of something, such
as an objective form, one cannot prove that that cognition is
verifying simply on the grounds that it has an object; nor can
one claim that that object exists simply on the grounds that
it is apprehended. That would be circular reasoning. The problem arises from the [Realists'] inability to establish the existence of an object and the verifiability of a cognition purely
on a conventional basis. Thus, to establish the validity of one
cognition, one would need another verifying cognition to apprehend it...and another would be needed to establish its
verifiability, *ad infinitum*. This is a fallacious approach.

Thus, the Idealist speaks of a self-ascertaining, verifying cognition that apprehends verifying cognitions. That cognition establishes the verifiability of cognitions. For example, the visual perception of form is dependent upon another object. But another type of awareness apprehends itself and does not depend upon another object: The seer and the seen are not different.

20. Such blue [-ness of a blue thing] is not regarded as
    the cause of [its own] blueness, as in the case of the
    non-blueness [of a crystal, where there *is* causation].
    What blue would make just blue, itself [made] by
    itself?

Centrist: The blueness of lapis lazuli is created by other conditions; it is not created by itself.

21. The statement that a lamp illuminates is made upon
    knowing this with awareness. The statement that the
    mind illuminates is made upon knowing this by what
    awareness?

Centrist: Upon analysis, a prior awareness does not apprehend an awareness in the present that has not yet arisen at the time of the prior cognition. A later awareness does not apprehend an awareness that has arisen and already passed. An awareness in the present cannot be both a subject and its own object. Thus, according to the system that asserts that the designated object[5] is found upon analysis, by means of what cognition is awareness said to be clear?

22. If nothing observes whether it is illuminating or not,
    to speak about it is foolish, as in the case of the beauty
    of a barren woman's daughter.

Centrist: We, who recognize the analytic unfindability of sought referents, maintain that there is no cognition that sees this; so one cannot state whether it is illuminating or not. It would be like speaking of the beauty of a barren woman's daughter—it is nowhere to be found.

Idealist: It is necessary that awareness illuminate itself, as stated above; and this assertion is needed to establish verifying cognition. Thus, there is self-cognizing awareness.[6]

23. [Idealist:] If there is no self-cognizing awareness, how is consciousness recalled?
    [Centrist]: Recollection is due to the connection with the perception of something else. This is like the poison of a rat ['s bite].

Idealist: In order for recollection to occur, there must be prior experience. Without prior experience, there can be no recollection. There is the twofold classification of "self-experience" and "other-experience." If the experience [of one's own consciousness] is an other-experience—i.e. an experience of some other entity—infinite regress ensues. Therefore, such experience must be self-experience [i.e. an awareness of an entity that is of the same nature as the awareness itself]. Thus, the experience must be one in which there is awareness of itself, otherwise recollection could not occur. For example, from a prior perception of blue, there later occurs the recollection of the object—blue—and the recollection of the subject—"I saw blue." Therefore, together with a prior experience of the object, there was self-cognizing awareness of the subject—the visual perception of blue. In that way there can occur a later recollection that "I saw blue."

Centrist: There is no need to experience something in order for it later to be recalled. For example, while one is unaware, one might be bitten and thereby poisoned by a rat. Although one experiences being bitten, one does not experience the invasion of the poison into one's body. Although that is not perceived, later, when the effects of the poison are felt, one recalls that while unaware, the poison was injected.

Likewise, due to the perception of blue, one later recalls the visual perception of blue; but for that to occur, it was not necessary for that perception to experience itself. How does that recollection arise? Upon experiencing the other object—blue— due to the connection between the subject and object, recollection [of the former] occurs. So there is no need first to experience the subject.

24. [Idealist]: In a different circumstance, [the minds of others] are seen, so [the mind must also] illuminate itself.
[Centrist]: A pot is seen due to the application of an empowered eye-ointment, but the ointment itself would not be seen.

Idealist: Upon attaining meditative quiescence, it is possible to perceive the minds of other distant people.[7] Thus, it must be possible for one's own mind to be perceived by itself.

Understand the specific point being refuted here. This refers to the refutation of the [Idealist's theory about] mind perceiving itself. For example, one must recall that it is possible to cultivate meditative quiescence which is focussed upon the mind.[8] This discussion concerns a single awareness perceiving itself. The Idealist argument, once again, is that if it is possible to observe the minds of other distant beings, there could be no flaw in the statement that awareness perceives itself, which is right at hand.

Centrist: The fact that one can see something distant does not necessarily imply that one can see something else close by. For example, by the use of a special eye-ointment it may be possible to observe a buried pot of treasure; but the ointment itself would not be seen.[9] According to our understanding of the analytic unfindability of sought referents, it is not possible for awareness to observe itself. When one analyzes former and later moments of awareness and seeks the designated object, it is not to be found. In this way, the Idealist presentation falls apart, i.e. it cannot be applied to reality.

Idealist: Do you Centrists refute the entire presentation of cognition, including the experiencing, seeing and hearing of events? If you take the above stance [with regard to self-cognizing awareness], this invalidates awareness.

25. Here that which is seen, heard and cognized is not refuted; rather, the conception [of them] as truly existent, which is the cause of suffering, is here to be prevented.

Centrist: With regard to cognition, if one seeks the designated object, it is not to be found. But [the cognized object] is not invalidated or refuted by such reasoning. Although it exists, if one seeks it with reasoning [by applying ultimate analysis], it is not found. It is not truly existent, so when reasoning seeks a truly existent entity, none is found. But the fact that it is not found under such analysis is not because it is simply non-existent.

This form of logical analysis has the purpose of eradicating the conception of true existence, which acts as the root of attachment and hostility and brings suffering to individuals.[10] It is reasoning entailing ultimate analysis. If that which is denied—an ultimately existent entity—did exist, then things would exist by their own mode of existence.[11] If that were the case, then when applying logical analysis, [truly existent] things should present themselves. The function of such analysis is to check whether entities exist by their own mode of existence or not; so if they do, that should be discovered by such analysis. But since such analysis yields a negative result, that reasoning repudiates ultimate, or true, existence. That is the difference between something not being found by reasoning, and something being invalidated by reasoning.

Here cognition is not repudiated; rather, the conception of true existence, which is the cause of suffering, is to be dispelled.

26. [Idealist]: Illusion is not different from the mind, neither is it regarded as non-different.
   [Centrist]: If it really exists, how can it be non-different

[from the mind]? If it is non-different [from the mind],
it does not exist in reality.

Idealist: Since external objects[12] do not exist, they are not
substantially distinct from the mind. Nor do they exist as mind.
Form and so on do not exist as external objects, but they are
not simply non-existent. They are not of a different nature than
the mind, nor are they the mind itself.

Centrist: If external objects truly exist, they would have to
exist in the manner in which they appear; and in that case,
they would have to be substantially different from the mind.
Now, if they are not substantially different, and if manifold
images[13] are truly of the nature of a single cognition, then those
images would be deceptive. In that case, the cognition would
not exist in reality. If they are not substantially different, they
would not truly exist.

27. [Idealist]: Although illusion is not truly existent, it is
    something observed.
    [Centrist]: Likewise, the mind [although not truly ex-
    istent] is an observer.
    [Idealist]: Cyclic existence has a basis in reality; other-
    wise, it would be like space.

Idealist: Forms and so forth appearing as external objects
are not truly existent; i.e. they do not exist as external objects.
They are devoid of such existence, and thus they are like illusions. Nevertheless, they are observed.

Centrist: In the same way, the mind, which is the observer,
appears to be truly existent, but is not. Thus, it too can be
regarded as illusion-like. So there is no need to assert the mind
as truly existent. Although external phenomena appear, they
are not truly existent; and thus they are considered to be
illusion-like. In the same manner, the observing mind appears
but is not truly existent; and it is therefore regarded as illusion-
like. Where is the fallacy in such reasoning?

Idealist: Cyclic existence, forms, imputed entities[14] and so on require a truly existent basis for their deceptive appearance. That is, each has to have a basis in reality. If they lacked such a basis, they would be like space. Thus, they would not be a source of either benefit or harm.

28. Since the dependence on reality is of a non-real [thing], could it have any efficiency? The mind, according to you, is reduced to a state of isolation without any accompaniment.

Centrist: If cyclic existence and so on, being unreal,[15] depended upon a real basis of their deceptive appearance, how could they have any function? You say that if they did not depend upon such a basis, they would not have the function of binding or liberating sentient beings; and there could be no alteration in that which has such a basis. Since there could be no change, there would be no bondage or liberation.

If there were no external objects, the mind, as you assert it, would be isolated in its own self-illuminating self-cognition, without the accompaniment of the dualistic, deceptive appearance of subject and object.

29. If the mind were separated from its apprehended object, then all beings would be Tathagatas. So what good is gained by regarding [entities] as mind only?

Centrist: If the mind were freed of the dualistic appearance of subject and object—e.g. in a state of meditative equipoise— then all sentient beings would be Tathagatas [Buddhas] long ago. By turning away from the basis of dualistic appearance, they would abide in the sphere of reality and would have become Tathagatas already.

If that were the case, what is the point in your setting forth the Mind-only view in order to escape the bondage of mental distortions?

3   The Necessity of the Centrist Path

THE NECESSITY OF REALIZING EMPTINESS

30. Even if one knows [something] to be like an illusion,
    how does this prevent mental distortions? Lust for an
    illusory woman may arise even in her creator.

Now the author presents rebuttals of criticisms of the Centrist view:

Objection: You Centrists present the view that all entities are like illusions; but by cultivating that understanding, one cannot avert mental distortions. It is evident that a magician may feel lust for his own creation of the illusion of a woman. So merely recognizing something as an illusion is not enough.

31. For that creator, the instincts of mental distortions toward objects have not been eliminated. Thus, when he sees [the illusory woman], his instinct for [understanding] emptiness is very weak.

Rebuttal: The creator of the illusion, upon seeing the attractive appearance of the illusory woman as truly existent, has not yet eradicated the instincts of mental distortions. So he grasps onto her true existence, and under that influence, mental distortions arise. Although he knows that the illusory woman is "empty" of existence as an actual woman, mental distortions arise with regard to her attractive appearance. Why? Because he still grasps onto the true existence of the illusory woman, and this leads to lust for her. Thus, the understanding of the emptiness of the illusory woman has not been deeply cultivated.

32. By building up instincts of [understanding] emptiness, the instincts of [grasping onto] reality are eliminated. And by cultivating [the realization that] nothing whatever is [truly existent], [the instinct for grasping onto the true existence of emptiness] too, will eventually be discarded.

If one builds up instincts for [understanding] emptiness by logically establishing all entities as being empty of true existence, experientially realizes this, and repeatedly enters into that experience, then the instincts for [grasping onto] reality can be dispelled.

If one perceives the absence of an intrinsic nature in forms and so on, then when such phenomena appear, they can be seen as deceptive, or not truly existent. Then when one looks upon attractive or unattractive phenomena, and attachment or aversion arise, one can actually ascertain that they do not truly exist—despite appearances to the contrary. This will diminish the occurrence of attachment and aversion, which result from the conception of events as existing in the manner in which they appear. This false way of apprehending things has been with us since beginningless time.

First one ascertains the lack of an intrinsic nature in forms and so on. When one gains an understanding of this emptiness of such things, one investigates the mode of existence of that emptiness. One finds that it, too, is devoid of intrinsic being and exists merely by the power of convention. This is the emptiness of emptiness. Emptiness itself is not truly existent.

Thus, first one investigates the ultimate nature of things such as forms, and by ascertaining their emptiness of intrinsic existence, craving and aversion toward them are decreased. Then one investigates the nature of emptiness and discovers it to have only conventional existence. As a result, one does not conceive of emptiness as being truly existent. Then when emptiness is ascertained, apart from cutting away the object of refutation, the mind does not conceive of anything. The mind stops with the sheer ascertainment of the absence of intrinsic existence and abides in that experience of emptiness, which is the absence of the object of refutation. There is no thought that "this is emptiness" or "this is the absence of intrinsic existence." There is only the awareness of the absence of intrinsic existence.

33. When something is not apprehended and it is considered as non-existent, then how can this non-entity, which has no foundation, remain before the mind?

When one is investigating an object to determine whether or not it is truly existent, one eventually arrives at the conclusion that the object does not exist in the way that it appears. At that moment, nothing appears before the mind except the emptiness that is the absence of the object of refutation. When this cognition wanes, one should repeatedly bring to mind the arguments for the lack of intrinsic existence and thus reinforce the strength of one's investigation. It is important to maintain the experience of the sheer emptiness of the object of refutation, i.e. the ascertainment of the absence of intrinsic existence.

34. When neither a [truly existent] entity nor a [truly existent] non-entity remains before the mind, then since there is no other alternative, [the mind,] being without the objective support [of grasping onto true existence], is calmed.

This stanza refers to the Path of Superior Beings.[1] By repeatedly cultivating the awareness of emptiness, one eventually realizes that all events are devoid of intrinsic existence. First one receives instruction in the appropriate treatises from a spiritual mentor. One thereby gains understanding based on the verses of the texts. This is understanding due to hearing. Then by patient investigation and repeated reflection there arises a sense of certainty due to reflection. This entails an understanding of the view that all entities are devoid of intrinsic existence.

Now in order to gain perfect certainty of the view, it is probably necessary to have the support of meditative concentration.[2] When the mind has little stability—or capacity of single-pointed concentration—it is unlikely that one could profoundly ascertain the absence of an intrinsic nature of all entities for longer than a fleeting instant. So one needs the aid of concentration. With that, one eventually gains understanding due to meditation, focussed on emptiness; and it is stable.

This is discussed in explanations of the Path of Preparation.[3] During the four successive stages of the Path of Preparation, dualistic appearance becomes increasingly subtle. Finally, at the initial moment of realization of emptiness on the Path of Seeing, all dualistic appearances, even the most subtle, are completely gone. Then, like water pouring into water, there occurs an experience with no sense of a distinction between subject and object.

By cultivating that realization, there finally occurs the diamond-like concentration[4] on the Path of Meditation. That acts as the direct remedy for cognitive obscurations, and omniscient wisdom arises. As long as one is not yet fully awakened, when non-conceptual, meditative realization of emptiness occurs, all conceptual elaborations are pacified. But dualistic appearance returns when one arises from meditation. However, once omniscient wisdom arises, all conceptual elaborations vanish, and they never recur. Then the attributes of the full fruition of the path of awakening arise.

35. Just as a wish-fulfilling gem and a wish-granting tree
   satisfy all desires, in the same way the image of the

Victor is considered [to fulfill all desires, motivated]
by the [needs of] disciples and the vows [of the
Awakened One].

Upon full awakening, the mind is not moved the tiniest bit
by conceptions of motivation and effort. However, by the force
of the merit of disciples and the Awakened Being's own previous altruistic prayers, the body of a Victor appears instantly
to disciples in pure and impure realms.[5] The body appears effortlessly, by the power of prayer.

36. If an alchemist dies after producing a pillar, even if
   a long time had passed since his death, it would still
   neutralize poisons and so on.

For example, even if a long time has passed since the death
of a brahmin who prepared a medicinal pillar, by the power
of his previous prayers, if one worships at that pillar, poisons
and so forth will be neutralized.[6]

37. Likewise, the "pillar" of the Victor's [body] is created
   in accordance with the Bodhisattva's deeds; and
   though the Bodhisattva has passed away, he [or she]
   still accomplishes all necessary works.

Also when the pillar [i.e. body] of the Victor is produced,
in accordance with the Bodhisattva's actions, all deeds are performed even though the Bodhisattva has passed away. These
are done effortlessly.

38. If [an Awakened Being has] no [conceptual] mind, how
   could worshiping [such a person] be fruitful? Because
   it is written that [the value is] equal whether [the
   Awakened Being] is present or passed away.

Since conceptualizing has vanished from the mind of a
Tathagata, how could it be helpful to worship such a being?

It is beneficial because it is said there is just as much value in worshiping a Buddha while he [or she] is present on earth as there is in worshiping the relics of such a being after he [or she] has passed into Nirvana.

39. Whether [that worship exists] conventionally or in reality, the scriptures [state that] there is a fruitful effect. It is, for example, like the fruitfulness of worshiping a truly existent Buddha.

Centrist: I maintain that the merit that accrues from worshiping an Awakened Being exists merely conventionally. You assert that it is truly existent. Either way, we agree that there is benefit in worshiping a Buddha who has passed into Nirvana. For example, you Realists believe that it is fruitful to worship a truly existent Buddha. I believe that illusion-like merits are accrued from the worship of an illusion-like Buddha. But we agree that such worship is fruitful.[7]

40. Liberation is gained from seeing [the Four Noble] Truths, so what is the point of perceiving emptiness? The scriptures state that there is no spiritual awakening without this path.

Shantideva declared previously that it is necessary to stop grasping onto true existence and to realize emptiness. Here is an objection:

In order to become omniscient, one must realize emptiness, but such realization is not needed simply to gain liberation from cyclic existence. By cultivating the path of wisdom of the Four Noble Truths, with their sixteen attributes, it is possible to dispel the mental afflictions that are brought on by grasping onto a self-sufficient, substantial personal identity. By subduing such afflictions one can attain liberation, so there is no need to meditate on emptiness.

Moreover, the view of emptiness that is included among the sixteen attributes of the Four Noble Truths is declared to be

the liberating path of wisdom. The other attributes are said
to be preparatory paths. Thus, by meditating on the emptiness and identitylessness that are included among the sixteen
attributes,[8] one can attain liberation. So what is the point of
meditating on emptiness [as it is set forth in the preceding
verses]?

Rebuttal: In many of the definitive discourses of the Buddha, it is said that if one grasps onto reality, lacking the view
of emptiness, there is no liberation. All the stages of awakening, from the stage of Stream Entry to becoming an Arhat,[9]
require realization of emptiness. Those sutras state that people wishing to follow the spiritual paths of Listeners, Solitary
Sages and Bodhisattvas should all train in transcendent wisdom. Thus, all three states of awakening are impossible without such realization.

41. Now it may be argued [by Hinayanists] that the Ma-
    hayana [scriptures] are not established [as the Buddha's
    teachings. In that case,] on what grounds is your own
    [Hinayana] canon so established?
    [Hinayanist]: Because it is granted authenticity by both
    of us.
    [Rebuttal]: Then yours was not authenticated from the
    start.

Objection: The scriptures cited above are Mahayana sources,
but it is doubtful whether those discourses are Buddha's words.
So you cannot prove your point by citing sutras whose authenticity is in question.

Rebuttal: If you deny that the Mahayana sutras are Buddha's
words, how do you so establish your Hinayana canon?[10]

Objection: The authenticity of our canon is not in doubt,
for both the Hinayanists and the Mahayanists agree on this.
You Mahayanists believe that your canon is authentic, whereas
we do not; but our canon is firmly established beyond question.

Rebuttal: In that case, at the time you were born—when you
did not yet believe in the Hinayana canon—it was not authen-

ticated, was it?

42. You should acknowledge that the grounds for your belief in that [Hinayana canon] also apply to the Mahayana. On the other hand, if something were true because two parties assert it, then the Vedas and so on would also be the truth.

The criteria for establishing certain teachings as being the Buddha's words are (1) the guidance contained in them is permitted in the Vinaya, (2) they relate to the Sutras and (3) they relate to and are not incompatible with the Abhidharma. Those criteria are satisfied for the Mahayana canon. If one assumes the authenticity of the Hinayana canon simply on the grounds that two parties—the Hinayanists and the Mahayanists—agree on this, then the Vedas would also be the truth.

43. [Objection]: Mahayana [is to be rejected since its authenticity] is contested.
[Rebuttal]: Then since [the validity of the entire Hinayana canon] is contested by non-Buddhists, and certain other [Hinayana] scriptures are contested by your own and other [Hinayana orders], reject them [too].

One might take the position that the Mahayana canon should be rejected since it is contested by Hinayanists. But that is a poor reason. The validity of the Hinayana canon as a whole is accepted by some and rejected by others. Moreover, non-Buddhists[11] do not believe in the Buddhist scriptures. So the validity of the Hinayana canon is also contested. Disagreement also occurs among Hinayana schools.

Thus, the contention that the Mahayana scriptures are not the Buddha's words is not only a contemporary issue. Arguments for the authenticity of the Mahayana are found in Shantideva's writings, in Nagarjuna's *Jewel Garland*[12] and in Maitreya's *Ornament for the Sutras*.[13] The fact that its authenticity has been contested is quite understandable. In the Mahayana sutras many extraordinary mysteries are discussed which the minds of ordinary beings like ourselves cannot fathom. When one fails to comprehend such explanations, one tends to doubt their validity.

Nevertheless, if only the Hinayana and not the Mahayana sutras were Buddha's teachings, then Buddhist spirituality would be impoverished by the absence of the latter. Moreover, if the Mahayana canon were not the Buddha's teachings, then one could ask whether it is possible to attain omniscience, or the state of Buddhahood, by means of the thirty-seven elements of the Hinayana path.[14] Even the Hinayana scriptures acknowledge the different spiritual paths of a Listener, a Solitary Sage and of a Bodhisattva.[15] How does one proceed on the Bodhisattva path? How is the awakening of a Buddha experienced? It would be exceedingly difficult to set out on that path solely on the basis of the Hinayana scriptures, without the Mahayana.

Most importantly, one cannot attain the Nirvana [of Buddhahood] solely on the basis of the Hinayana treatises, nor can one realize emptiness. Without realization of emptiness, Nirvana cannot be attained, in which case the "Truth of Cessation" is reduced to mere talk. Thus, if the authenticity of the Mahayana is not established, it is virtually impossible to grant the authenticity of the Hinayana.

Now it is well known in Buddhist tradition that historically three compilations of the Buddha's teachings occurred. On the first occasion, the three "baskets" of the Buddha's teachings[16] were assembled, and there is no reference to a Mahayana compilation. In the celebrated, early historical accounts there is no mention of the Mahayana, and this gives rise to questions. But I do not think this is problematic.

The widely celebrated teachings that the historical Buddha gave in India are the Hinayana discourses. But apart from those, I believe he gave Mahayana teachings to a small number of beings who were pure in action.[17] For example, it is unlikely that Vultures Peak in India was massive during the time of the Buddha, whereas now it is quite small. It was probably the same size then. However, in the Mahayana sutras there are accounts of the Buddha teaching on Vultures Peak in the midst of thousands of Arhats and hundreds of thousands of Bodhisattvas. It would seem that there would not be room for such an assembly. Let alone the gods in the congregation, who have subtler bodies, there is not sufficient space on that little hill to accomodate even that number of human beings. So I do not think they were all assembled on that hill as we perceive it.

When the Buddha gave Mahayana teachings there, they were heard by disciples who were pure in action; and to them that site appeared broad and vast. The Buddha did not offer Mahayana teachings to the general public; they would not have been of benefit. His most public, or celebrated, discourses were given in the presence of such Listeners as Shariputra and Maudgalyayana. In the circle of his disciples who were pure in action were Maitreya, Manjushri and so on—Bodhisattvas who appeared in the form of gods. To such disciples the Buddha appeared to teach in the presence of these beings as well as Listener disciples.

Now to the smallest number of disciples of extraordinarily pure action the Buddha gave tantric teachings.[18] To some such disciples he generated a mandala with himself as the deity within it, engaging in meditative concentration on the nonduality of the profound and the vivid reality;[19] but the chief deity in the mandala appeared in the form of the Buddha as a monk. Then the even subtler mysteries were taught to disciples of even greater purity who, by practicing higher forms of method and wisdom, gained realization of non-dual ultimate and phenomenal reality. For such disciples there were no obstructions to the Buddha casting off the form of a monk and appearing as a richly adorned deity or as a World Monarch.[20] For them it was very meaningful for the Buddha to appear in such guises.

It is not possible for gross consciousness to transform into omniscient wisdom; only a subtle mind can be so transformed.

To facilitate this the Buddha revealed practices to focus the mind on the channels, energies and drops of the subtle human anatomy.[21] These were given only to those disciples of the utmost purity.

Thus, to disciples of increasing purity, ability and rarity the Buddha gave more private guidance in the subtle mysteries. It appears that such teachings are included in the Mahayana sutras. There is no certainty, however, that all of the tantras were taught while the historical Buddha was alive. To an extremely small number of pure disciples the Buddha could appear today. They could encounter Vajradhara, the King of the Tantras, and he could reveal tantras and quintessential guidance to them. This is possible even though more than twenty-five hundred years have gone by since the historical Buddha passed away. There is no possibility, after the Buddha's death, of additions being made to his public discourses. But I think that teachings to disciples of pure action do not necessarily have to be given during the historical Buddha's lifetime. That is my opinion.

Nowadays there are people who object to the terms "Mahayana" and "Hinayana." They regard the latter term, meaning "Lesser Vehicle," as pejorative, or disparaging, and declare this to be a source of discord among Buddhists. This is something to be considered. The distinction of "Great Vehicle" and "Lesser Vehicle" was not made to demonstrate contempt for the latter. Followers of the Mahayana should study and practice the Hinayana teachings. The distinction between the two Vehicles is made in terms of their differing presentations of (1) the basis of spiritual practice, (2) the extent of the motivation and practice along the spiritual path and (3) the degrees of awakening due to differing levels of purity and realization. Thus, the terms were not created out of disrespect or sectarianism. Basically there is nothing wrong with these labels, though they have become somewhat uncomfortable to use. For this reason there are people who think we should dispense with them.

We did not create these two terms. They are found in the

great Buddhist treatises of classical India, and the Buddha himself used them frequently, as recorded in the Mahayana sutras. If this dual classification is deemed fallacious, it is not we today who are in error; it rather implies that the Buddhist classics are at fault and that the Buddha was sectarian. So I do not think there is any point in dispensing with these terms.

Some people suggest that we use the terms "Listener Vehicle," "Solitary Sage Vehicle" and "Bodhisattva Vehicle." Those are found in the Hinayana scriptures and they are in accord with the Mahayana. Thus, one could simply not use the former two terms and use these three instead, without condemning the former.

44. You might insist that the root of the teachings is the monastic community. But it is implausible that those monks [were Arhats]. For those whose minds are subject to grasping [onto true existence], Nirvana is implausible.

Now begins a logical argument for the authenticity of the Mahayana. Without the view of emptiness as it is revealed in the Mahayana sutras, it is impossible to attain any of the three states of awakening. If one takes the position that the root of the teachings is the monks who are Arhats, Shantideva replies: If those monks do not assert emptiness, they could not be Arhats. Why? Because if one lacks realization of emptiness, mental distortions cannot be eliminated; and if they are not eliminated, one cannot become an Arhat. Thus, the root of the teachings could not be monk Arhats.

In short, if the mind is still subject to grasping onto true existence, Nirvana cannot be attained.

45. You may say that by eliminating mental distortions, they would immediately be liberated. But for them the effectiveness of tainted action is still in evidence, even without mental distortions [as explained in the Abhidharma].

Vaibhashika: Those monks would indeed be Arhats, for by meditating on the sixteen attributes of the Four Noble Truths as explained in the Abhidharma treatises, the mental distortions can be eliminated. And by eliminating them, liberation is gained.[22]

Centrist: That is incorrect. You maintain that the subtle state of mind that grasps onto the intrinsic nature of entities is in accord with reality. You fundamentally assume that all entities are truly existent. You believe that it is realistic to apprehend phenomena according to the way they appear—viz. as truly existent. You explain mental distortions such as attachment and hostility in terms of those that are produced by grasping onto a self-sufficient, substantial self. Those are far grosser mental distortions [than those resulting from grasping onto true existence]. Merely eliminating the gross mental distortions explained in the Abhidharma entails a temporary eradication of active distortions. That is insufficient for becoming an Arhat.

Because those gross distortions are isolated from certain conditions, they do not arise. However, subtle attachment and hostility resulting from subtle grasping onto true existence are not even temporarily suppressed. They are active, and as a result, tainted action is accumulated by that degree of craving and grasping. That power of tainted action is seen both by reasoning and on the basis of scriptural authority.

There are a few people in Burma nowadays who are regarded as Arhats. Now I am not able to gauge their level of realization, but my opinion is that they have temporarily suppressed the active mental distortions that are explained in the Abhidharma. As a result, gross attachment and hostility do not arise, and for that reason they are widely regarded as Arhats. If they have realized subtle emptiness, they could indeed be actual Arhats. If not, they would be Arhats as described in the Abhidharma. But in terms of the [Centrist] system that considers grasping onto true existence as a mental distortion, they would not be Arhats.

46. You may object that as long as craving, which clings

[to existence] is absent, [liberation] is certain. Although that craving is not afflicted [by grasping onto an independent self], why could it not be similar to confusion?

You [Vaibhashikas] maintain that craving, which grasps onto the aggregates of the body and mind, has been eliminated. However, although craving, as it is described in the Abhidharma, does not appear, the subtle craving that results from grasping onto true existence has not been eliminated. It, too, is a mental affliction.

According to your [Vaibhashika] system there is a twofold classification of confusion: one is a mental distortion and the other is not. Likewise, there is a form of craving that you do not recognize as being a mental distortion.

47. Craving arises from feeling, and feeling is found in those [people you regard as Arhats]. They remain with a mind subject to grasping [onto the true existence] of some things.

If feelings occur in which one grasps onto true existence, craving will arise. Briefly stated: As long as one grasps onto the true existence of objects, the mental distortion of craving will continue to arise.

48. In a mind lacking [realization of] emptiness, the fetters arise again, just as in the case of non-conscious meditative equipoise. Thus, one should meditate on emptiness.

As long as one lacks realization of emptiness, the active occurrence of mental distortions, or fetters, may be temporarily suspended; but when the appropriate conditions are eventually encountered, they will arise again. As a result of non-conscious meditative equipoise,[23] gross mental distortions temporarily do not manifest; but they recur when contributing circumstances are met. Likewise, as long as one has not eliminated subtle grasping onto true existence [by realizing subtle emptiness], even though gross distortions are temporarily suspended, they will arise again when the appropriate conditions are met. Thus, one should definitely meditate on emptiness.

49. You may say that those utterances that correspond to the sutras are acknowledged as the Buddha's words. Why then do you not approve of the Mahayana, most of which is similar to [your] revered sutras?

It is said that the three verses beginning with this one were not composed by Shantideva, for their placing in the text is inappropriate and they denigrate Mahakashyapa.[24] If they did belong in the text, they should appear at the end of the arguments for the authenticity of the Mahayana [i.e. following vs. 44].

In any case, the point of this verse is that since most of the Mahayana sutras are similar to the Hinayana sutras, the former should also be acknowledged as the Buddha's teachings.

50. If the entire [Mahayana canon] is corrupt because of one exception, since one [Mahayana] sutra is comparable to [the Hinayana canon], why are they not all spoken by the Victor?

If one concludes that all the Mahayana sutras are corrupt on the grounds that one of them does not meet the criteria for being Buddha's words, then one could equally claim that all are authentic on the grounds that one of them meets those criteria.

51. This is a doctrine whose depths were not fathomed even by Mahakashyapa. Who then would refuse to accept it simply because you fail to understand it?

In terms of common appearances, Mahakashyapa and others

did not fathom the Mahayana sutras. So who would say that they are not to be accepted simply because you do not understand them?

52. [The Bodhisattvas'] presence in the cycle of existence for the sake of those suffering due to confusion is brought about by [their] freedom from attachment and fear. This is the result of [realizing] emptiness.

A person who has realized emptiness does not remain in the cycle of existence due to attachment, or the power of mental distortions and actions conditioned by them. Nor does he [or she] fall to the extreme of seeking annihilation due to fear of the cycle of existence. How can one eternally serve the needs of sentient beings? This, says the author, comes as a result of realizing emptiness.

One needs to integrate the spirit of awakening and the practice of wisdom, viz. the realization of emptiness. In this way, due to wisdom one does not abide in the cycle of existence, and due to compassion one does not abide in tranquility [i.e. Nirvana]. With those two qualities, it is said, it is possible to serve the needs of sentient beings forever. This seems to imply that great compassion is also a fruit of realizing emptiness.

53. Thus, since no refutation can be produced with regard to emptiness, there is no doubt that realization of emptiness is to be cultivated.

54. The antidote to the darkness of afflictive obscurations and cognitive obscurations is [the realization of] emptiness. Why do those [who desire to attain] omniscience not swiftly cultivate it?

55. Let fear appropriately arise toward something that produces suffering; but since [realization of] emptiness pacifies suffering, why should it be dreaded?

As explained above, grasping onto true existence acts as the basis for the occurrence of attachment and hostility. One may fear such grasping, which produces suffering; but it is inappropriate to dread [the realization of] emptiness, which is the antidote for such grasping and which pacifies suffering.

56. If there were some entity called "I," there could be
    fear due to anything. But if there is no such thing as
    even the self, whose fear will there be?

If there were an "I" that existed by its own independent nature, then at times of fear one would grasp onto that self, and attachment and hostility would arise. When ordinary people experience fear, there is attachment to the self, thinking, "Poor *me!*". But if there is no such self, who is there to experience fear?

**Part Two:
Identitylessness**

4 Personal Identitylessness

REFUTATION OF AN INTRINSIC "I"

Now begins an explanation of personal identitylessness.[1] Up
to this point we have presented emptiness as it is discussed
in the Centrist treatises. It was shown that this is the most
profound theory of emptiness. Idealists assert phenomenal
identitylessness,[2] but they regard this merely as the absence
of external objects. They explain phenomenal identitylessness
as follows: "Form does not exist by its own identity as the
basis of the concept of form. But such an approach is insufficient for ascertaining subtle emptiness, viz. the lack of intrinsic existence. Thus, the Idealists' way of asserting emptiness
is refuted.

Then Shantideva argues that the realization of emptiness is
indispensable, regardless of one's spiritual "vehicle," be it that
of the Listeners, Solitary Sages or Bodhisattvas. Such insight
is said to be like the mother of spiritual awakening.

Then in terms of actually meditating on emptiness, the twofold distinction of personal and phenomenal identitylessness
is made with regard to the types of entities [whose ultimate
nature is emptiness]. There is no difference in subtlety between these two types of emptiness. The discussion of per-

sonal identitylessness comes first because emptiness is easier to ascertain with regard to the person [than to other phenomena].

When one says there is no self[3] of a person, the basis of that attribute [of identitylessness] is the person, and the point is that a person has no intrinsic self. In order to ascertain that identitylessness, one must recognize the identity, or self, in question. If its appearance is not clear to the mind, using scripture and reasoning, one will not be able to realize its non-existence.[4]

While dreaming, all kinds of things may come to mind, but these are nothing more than appearances. Likewise, a magician may create a variety of illusory appearances, but they do not exist objectively. Likewise, oneself, others, the cycle of existence, and liberation—in short, all entities—exist merely by the power of mind and convention. In no way do they exist independently from the side of the basis of designation.[5] While actually existing by the power of mind and convention, their mode of appearance is otherwise: Due to our habituation to ignorance since time without beginning, whatever good or bad things that appear to our six types of consciousness[6] do not at all seem to exist by the power of subjective convention. Everything *appears* to exist from the side of its basis of imputation. That mode of existence that accords with such a deceptive manner of appearance is the subtle object of refutation. Thus, it is to be totally repudiated by means of scripture and reasoning.

Whatever good or bad things appear to us seem to exist from the side of those objects. How do they exist? If they exist from the side of the object, then, contemplating the basis of imputation, which lies out there at finger-point, we should see whether it is the object in question or not. Let us take for example a physical object and examine its shape, color and so on to see if that object is to be found anywhere among those attributes. If we do so, we find nothing that is the object in question. If we take a person as an example, and inspect the individual aggregates that are the bases of designation of a person, we find that none of them is the person. In that way we recognize that the imputed object[7] is not to be found upon investigation.

Then if we contemplate how things appear to the mind, we see that they seem to exist from the side of the object, without dependence upon anything else. But when they are sought analytically, they are not found. They do exist, for they can help or harm us. But when pondering the manner in which they exist, we find no basis for the assumption that they exist from the side of the object. Thus, they exist by the power of subjective convention, by the power of designation.

When pondering the nature of existence, we find that entities are not found upon seeking them analytically. So they exist by means of conventional, conceptual designation. They do undeniably exist. But as long as they do not exist independently, from their own side, they must exist by the power of subjective convention. There is no alternative. An entity exists due to its being designated upon something that is not it.

First we need to understand that. Then we should see how things appear to the mind. In this way we should alternate between engaging in the above analysis and inspecting the manner in which events appear. If we integrate these two approaches, eventually whatever appears to the mind will be recognized as seeming to exist not due to convention, but to exist from the side of the object. This mode of appearance, entailing the thing to be refuted, will be clearly ascertained. Then when we apply reasoning to refute the true existence that accords with that mode of appearance, it will be helpful.

Whatever events appear to us now seem to exist from the side of the object, as if there is something out there to which we can point a finger. When we say, "This exists, that exists," pointing a finger here and there, it appears that those things exist from their own side without dependence upon anything else. They seem to exist independently. When we say "identitylessness," the "identity" in question is something existing in that way. The term "intrinsic nature" has the same meaning, as does "independent existence" and "true existence." Since that is non-existent, all entities lack true existence, they do not exist by their own intrinsic nature, or exist independently. They are identityless.[8]

As it says in Nagarjuna's *Jewel Garland*, there undeniably exists a person, a self, who engages in actions, experiences their results, who is the agent in the cycle of existence and in liberation. There is an "I" that exists in dependence upon the body and mind. If one investigates how the self exists, not being uncritically satisfied with the mere appearance of the self, one looks to the aggregates that are the basis upon which it is imputed. One checks whether the person is to be found in the "earth element" [the solid components of the body], the "water element" [the liquid components] and so on. Upon inspection, the self is not in evidence in the elements of earth, water, fire, air or space, or in all of them together. Nowhere among any of the physical constituents is the self identified. Moreover, there is no self that is of a nature distinct from the aggregates; for if there were, it would be unrelated to them. One could not say "my aggregates" [e.g. "my body and mind"].

Yet the self does indeed exist; and its location must be the mental and physical aggregates. It could not exist apart from them. However, not any one of those aggregates, nor the assembly of all of them, nor the continuum that they have in common, nor the individual continuum of any one of them can be identified as being the self.

Some great thinkers, such as Bhavaviveka, identify mental consciousness as the "I." But if one logically analyzes this and applies the word "I" to the mind, this would yield an expression equivalent to "the mind's mind" when saying "my mind." This mistakenly equates the actor and the action. Thus, consciousness cannot be identified as the self. In short, nothing whatever among the four physical elements, space or consciousness is found to be the self. Nothing is so identified by the Awakened Beings or by oneself, nor will the self be found in the future.

Nevertheless, the self exists, and its location could be nowhere but the aggregates of the person. But when those aggregates are individually examined, nothing is identified as the self. Thus, the self can only be something merely conceptually designated upon the mental and physical aggregates. And yet, when it appears to the mind, it does not seem to be a mere conceptual designation upon the aggregates; rather it appears to exist objectively.

57. The teeth, hair and nails are not I, nor am I bone, blood, mucus, phlegm, pus or lymph.

58. Bodily oil is not I, nor is sweat, fat or the entrails either. The cavity of the entrails is not I, nor is excrement or urine.

59. Flesh is not I, nor are the sinews, warmth nor air. The bodily cavities are not I, nor is any one of the six types of consciousness.

If the self truly exists in the manner in which it appears, then it should be identifiable as one inspects the components of a person one by one. Following the above verses, no part of the body, including the four elements and space, nor the six types of consciousness can be identified as the self. This implies that the self that experiences joy and sorrow and that appears to the mind as if it existed independently does not exist at all. This is ascertained by engaging in such analysis.

REFUTATION OF THE SAMKHYA THEORY OF SELF

60. If the awareness of sound [were the permanent self], sound would always be apprehended. In the absence of an object of awareness, what, do you say, would be known by what awareness?

In early times there were several non-Buddhist philosophical systems in India, including the Samkhya, Jaina, Vedanta and so on. I do not know if all of them still exist. Among them, the Samkhya system is one of the most profound. Here is a critique of the Samkhya theory of the self.[9]

Centrist: If a person, who is asserted to be awareness, and who experiences sound and so forth, is declared to be permanent [in the sense of being immutable] and partless, the person would have to apprehend sound at all times, even when there is no sound to be heard. Thus, it is incorrect to assert a permanent awareness, for [if there were ever awareness of sound,] it would have to be heard all the time. On the other hand, if there were no object of cognition, in this case sound, what is cognized so that you can even speak of cognition? If nothing is cognized, there can be no cognition.

61. If you assert that awareness exists in the absence [of an object of cognition], then it would follow that a piece of wood could be awareness. Thus, it is certain that without an object of awareness present, there is no awareness.

Centrist: If, even in the absence of sound, the awareness of sound could still exist—implying the existence of awareness with no object—a piece of wood could also be awareness. Thus, there can be no awareness of sound if no sound is present.

62. If that very [awareness] cognizes visual form, why does it not hear sound as well? If you reply that this sound is not nearby, then awareness of that would also not exist.

Centrist: Since awareness of sound is associated with sound, in the absence of the latter, the former cannot be posited. But according to the Samkhya system, a person is awareness and is permanent; thus, if a person ever heard sound, there could be no time when sound was not heard. So when a person cognizes visual form, while there is no sound present, there would also have to be awareness of sound.

Samkhya: In such a case, due to the absence of sound, there would be no awareness of sound.

Centrist: That, however, repudiates your assertion that the awareness of sound has a permanent nature. If it exists at one time and not at another, there is no way to assert that a [permanent] person [identified with that awareness] exists.

63. How can something that is the substance of the apprehending of sound be a cognition of visual form? A single [person] may be regarded as either a father or as a son, but this is not in terms of reality, (only relativistically).

Centrist: It is not possible that something that is the substance of apprehending sound could also be the substance of apprehending visual form. Those two substances could not be the same.

Samkhya: With regard to "perturbation"[10] and "substance,"[11]—when a single person apprehends visual form, he lacks the perturbation of sound but still has the substance of sound. So even when he sees form, there is no contradiction in asserting that he is a subject who apprehends sound. This is like regarding the same person as either a father [of his children] or a son [of his father], depending on the perspective.

Centrist: One may designate a single person as a father or as a son, but this is purely a matter of convention. This is not possible if one presumes to speak of intrinsic reality [as it is defined in the Samkhya or any other system].

64. For neither sattva, rajas nor tamas is either the son or the father. Moreover, the substance of [visual perception] is not seen to entail cognition of sound.

Samkhya: "Sattva"[12] refers to "joy," "rajas"[13] to "suffering," and "tamas"[14] refers to "confusion."[15] These three universal constituents[16] in equilibrium constitute the primal substance of the cosmos.[17] That is the substance[18] of phenomena, and it is regarded as ultimate truth.[19] This ultimate substance is never seen in the world of phenomena, and phenomena that are seen are regarded as illusion-like and deceptive. Thus, the primal substance in the case of the son is not the son, nor in the case of the father is it the father.[20]

Moreover, the substance of the cognition of visual form is not seen to be the substance of the cognition of sound, i.e. they are not seen to be identical.

65. But if [the cognition of visual form is the cognition of sound] in another form, like an actor, then it is not permanent. If [the cognition of form] is another cognition, then that singularity is unprecedented.

Centrist: If one substance takes on different forms, then it is incorrect to say that it is permanent [in the sense of "unchanging"]. A permanent substance that is identical with something whose form changes is unprecedented. There could not be a truly existent substance that takes a variety of forms. Such an entity would have to be unreal.

66. If you claim that the other mode [of cognition] does not truly exist, then say what its natural form is. If you reply, "Consciousness itself," then it entails the [unwanted] consequence that all conscious beings are identical.

Centrist: If you say that another mode [of a certain cognition] does not truly exist in the manner in which it appears, but exists as a single substance, tell us what that intrinsic nature, or substance, is. If you claim that consciousness itself is truly existent, then it would follow that all beings are one. Since all beings with different continua would have such a nature, it would follow that they would all be identical.

67. That which has volition and that which lacks it would

be the same, because their very being is equivalent. If a specific entity is deceptive, what corresponding basis does it have?

Centrist: If multiple entities are alike in all respects due to a single similarity, then things that have and do not have volition would be the same, for they are alike in their very being. If specific, distinct perturbations, such as visual cognition and audial cognition, are false, or deceptive, since they are similar, what is their corresponding, truly existent primal substance?

REFUTATION OF THE NYAYA THEORY OF THE SELF

68. That which is not conscious is not I, because it lacks consciousness, just like a cloth and so on. If you counter that it is conscious since it is conjoined with consciousness, then it would follow that the non-conscious entity would vanish.

Naiyayika: We deny the existence of a self that is of the nature of awareness. Rather, in a person's being there is an immutable, partless, pervasive material entity that lacks volition but nevertheless experiences the world and engages in action. That entity is the self.[22]

Centrist: An unconscious material substance is not an experiencing self because it lacks consciousness, just like a pot and so on.

Naiyayika: Although the self is an unconscious material entity, since it is endowed with consciousness, it is aware of things.

Centrist: Then when that consciousness becomes of the nature of the self, the previously unconscious self would change. In that case it could not be immutable.

69. Moreover, if the self is not subject to change, then what is the use of its consciousness? Thus, lacking consciousness and being separate from activity, space could

be regarded as the self.

Centrist: If the self is immutable, partless and pervasive, what effect could consciousness have on that material entity? Moreover, since you assert that the self is of a material nature, devoid of consciousness and divorced from activity, you may as well declare that space is the self.

REBUTTAL OF ARGUMENTS AGAINST IDENTITYLESSNESS

70. One might say that in the absence of a self there would be no proper relationship between an action and its result. If the agent vanishes upon having performed an action, who will [experience] this result?

The author previously argues that there does not exist a self that conforms to the way it is conceived when we grasp onto true existence. He then repudiates the speculative, non-Buddhist concept of the self as being permanent, partless and independent.[23] Now he presents an objection to the Centrist theory of the self.

Objection: If the self does not exist, then there is no way to assert any relationship between action and its result. Why? Because the time of engaging in an action and the time of experiencing its result are distinct. If one has committed a deed as a human being, it is possible to experience its results later in a non-human existence. Thus, if a self who has the same being is not acknowledged for those two existences, since they have different bodies and different minds [which are dependent on each body], there would be no relation between an action and its fruition.

The composite of the body and mind at the time of performing an action vanishes. When the effect of that action is experienced, another composite of body and mind has formed. So when the fruition of the act is experienced, whose fruition is it?

71. Since we both agree that an action and its fruition have different bases, and that the self who performs the action does not function at the time [of its fruition], is it not pointless to dispute this issue?

Response: The person at the time of performing an act and the person at the time of experiencing its result exist at different times and are of different natures. We both agree on this point. Neither of us believes that the self that experiences the effect is the self that engaged in the action. So there is no point in debating this issue.

72. It is not possible that the very possessor of the cause can be seen to be "endowed with the effect." Rather, agent and experience are designated depending on their oneness of continuum.

At the very time that a cause is created it is impossible for there to be an experience of the effect of that cause. The "self" is designated upon a continuum of consciousness. In this way one can say, "In a previous life I committed an action, and now I am experiencing its result."

The self that existed yesterday and the self today are different. Yesterday's self has passed, and today's self has newly arisen, but they are of the same continuum. Thus it is correct to say, "Today I experience the results of what I did yesterday."

73. The past or future mind is not the "I," for it is not found. Moreover, the present mind is not the self; [for if it were,] upon its passing, the self, too, would not exist.

If the self is designated upon the continuum of consciousness, one might well ask if consciousness itself is the self. The answer is in the negative. The past and future mind is not the self because it does not exist. When speaking of the past, future and present, the past has ceased and the future is yet to come. Roughly speaking, i.e. in terms of convention, it is possible to talk of the three times. But more precisely, if one distinguishes the past and future with regard to individual earlier and later moments, the former belong to the past and the latter to the future. The present is not to be found.[24] Thus, the present mind is not the self, for as soon as it had passed, the self would become non-existent.

74. When the trunk of a banana tree is cut into pieces,
    there is nothing left over. Just so, the "I" is not [found
    to be] really existent, when sought after analytically.

As it says in the *Jewel Garland*, if one cuts apart the trunk of a banana tree, which has no core, it is found to have no essence. Likewise, if one seeks the self, no entity can be found that is the self.

75. You might ask: If no sentient being is found, towards
    whom would one feel compassion? For practical pur-
    poses [one feels compassion for beings] who are im-
    puted by acknowledged delusion.

Objection: Now when one seeks the designated object, the self is not to be found. The terms "self," "person" and "individual" are equivalent, and the entity so designated is not to be identified. One cultivates compassion by reflecting, "People wish to be free of suffering, yet they are in pain. Might they be free of misery!" But if the person for whom one feels compassion is not to be found, to whom is the compassion directed?
Response: As it states in the *Jewel Garland*, due to ignorance as the cause, tainted actions are performed and beneficial and detrimental results follow. That ignorance is not to be denied, for it yields both benefit and harm. Sentient beings are not identifiable by analysis, but without such examination they evidently engage in actions and experience their pleasant and

painful results. One must acknowledge the explanation of the effects that ensue from ignorance. However, one does not assert them as truly [i.e. intrinsically] existent. They exist merely by the force of convention, without examination or analysis. The "delusion" that is referred to above does not refer to grasping onto true existence. Rather, it refers to delusion as it is popularly conceived, entailing no examination or analysis.

There do exist sentient beings, who give help and inflict pain. When saying that they exist only conventionally, the meaning is that they are not found under analysis; so they do not ultimately, or truly, exist. That which does exist does so by the force of convention, as a name; and it is deceptive, like an illusion. Its existence is established by deceptive but nevertheless verifying cognition.[25]

There is no way to establish the existence of anything unless one refrains from [ultimate] examination and analysis. However, it is necessary to draw a distinction between a person who appears in a dream and one who is encountered when one is awake. They are similar insofar as both are not truly existent. But if the former is designated as a person, this is repudiated by other conventional cognitions. If the latter is designated as a person, this is not contradicted by such cognitions, nor is it repudiated by ultimate analysis. Thus, such a being exists conventionally as a person.

If something is not repudiated by other conventional cognitions, nor by ultimate analysis, it may be asserted to exist. But there is nothing that exists on its own. There is no such mode of existence.

76. You may ask: If there is no sentient being, whose is the goal? We grant that such desire [for liberation, etc.] is indeed delusive. Still, in order to eradicate suffering, effective delusion, whose result [is understanding of the ultimate] is not prevented.

Objection: If sentient beings do not exist, who is it that attains the fruition of the spiritual path—full awakening? And while on the path, for whom does one cultivate compassion?

Response: Sentient beings do exist. It is for them that compassion is felt, and compassion is cultivated by existent people. Whatever is designated by delusion [as it was described above] is to be acknowledged. Due to cultivating compassion while on the spiritual path, the fruition of full awakening is attained. Who attains awakening? That, too, is to be established conventionally, without [ultimate] examination or analysis. In order to pacify the suffering of oneself and others, impure appearances that arise due to ignorance are not to be rejected.

77. Grasping onto the "I," which is a cause of suffering, is strengthened due to delusion about the self. You may think that you cannot get rid of it, [but for this,] meditation on selflessness is ideal.

The mental affliction of grasping onto the "I" is a cause of suffering.[26] One may doubt that there is any way to overcome that affliction; but it is indeed possible, and for this, meditation on identitylessness is ideal.

5 *Phenomenal Identitylessness*

THE FOUR APPLICATIONS OF MINDFULNESS

Mindfulness of the body
In the explanation of phenomenal identitylessness, the author
discusses the four applications of mindfulness on (1) the body,
(2) the feelings, (3) the mind and (4) other phenomena. Those
four subjects are brought under examination and are established as not truly existent. Thus, the conventional nature of
those four is not investigated; rather, mindfulness is applied
to their ultimate mode of existence.

78. The body is not the feet, the calves, nor the thighs;
    nor is it the hips, the abdomen, the back, the chest
    or the arms.

79. It is not the hands, the sides of the torso, the armpits
    or the shoulders; nor is the neck or head the body.
    So what here is the body?

If the self is imputed in dependence upon the body and
mind, what then is the nature of the body? We say "my body"
and "human body," and such designations are made upon the

collection of the feet, head, hands and so on. If one asks whether any individual component such as the head or a hand is the body, the answer must be "no." For if each part were the body, then a person would have many bodies. If quite a few of the parts are missing, it seems that there is not a body, but if only one is missing, the body still seems to be there. This is a matter of convention. If it seems inappropriate to make the designation of "body," it appears that there is no body; but if the designation is made, then there is a body. This is not determined by some presumably objective reality.

In terms of the author's analysis, the feet and so on are the parts, and a single human body is that which has those components. The "whole," the body, is imputed in dependence upon its parts. None of those parts can be identified as being the body.

80. If this body occurs partially in all [of the parts], and the parts occur in [all] the parts, where then can this [body as a whole] stand itself?

Hypothesis: The body, as the whole, is distinct from its individual parts, and it pervades all of them part by part.

Response: You may assert that the body as the whole exists in each of its components, but this suggests that the body itself is not composed of parts. Where then does it exist?

81. If the body were itself wholly located everywhere among the hands and so on, there would be just as many bodies as there are hands, etc.

If the whole body were located in each of the parts, there would be as many whole bodies as there are parts of the body, including the hands and so forth.

82. As the body does not [intrinsically] exist in the interior or on the exterior [of its parts], how can it exist among the hands and so on? As it is not distinct from [each

of its parts, including] the hands, etc., how can it exist at all?

When one seeks the imputed object, the body itself is not found either inside or on the surface of the parts. Since no independent, truly existent body is found, how can it exist among those parts? As the body is not of a different nature from its parts, then that designated object is not to be found.

83. While the body does not [intrinsically] exist, due to delusion there occurs a cognition of [an intrinsically existent] body among the hands and so on. This is like apprehending a pillar as being a person due to a certain configuration.

Thus, although there is no intrinsically existent body, on the basis of the components, including the hands and so on, a self-defining body appears to the mind. This is like looking on a pillar in the shape of a human and mistaking it for a human.

84. As long as there is the complex of conditions, the body [appears] as if it were a man. Likewise, as long as the hands and so on are present, the body is seen there.

On the basis of the assembly of the parts of the body one says "my body," "a good body" and "a poor body." In such cases the body seems clearly to exist from its own side. In fact the body is no more than a name which is designated on a certain basis, but it seems quite different from that.

85. Likewise, what would a hand be, [other] than an assemblage of fingers, or a [finger other] than a configuration of joints, or a joint [other than] its own separate parts?[2]

Previously there was an analysis of the body as a whole, and now the author discusses its components [e.g. the hands], the parts of those components [e.g. the fingers] and so on. "Hand" is imputed upon the configuration of the fingers, the palm and so on, but the hand does not exist among those individual parts. And there is no hand existing independently of those separate parts. Likewise, "finger" is designated upon a configuration of joints, and the joints, too, have their own separate parts.

86. Those parts, too, [exist only] due to the different atoms, and even the atoms [exist only] due to the divisions of their directional facets. Since those directional facets have no [intrinsic] parts, they are [like] space. Thus, the atom does not [intrinsically] exist.

One can likewise divide a joint into its most basic components, atoms;[3] and it, too, is not found among them. Once again the whole is designated in dependence on those components, but it is not found to exist independently.[4]

An atom can be analytically divided into its directional components—its eastern quadrant, etc. It, too, is not found among those separate parts. If one analytically tries to break down the directional facets into something else, one finds nothing at all. Or one can analyze them [into smaller directional facets] and come to the same conclusion that they have no intrinsic parts. In short, nothing can exist that is devoid of parts or attributes. When one investigates in that way, even atoms are not to be found.[5]

87. What discerning person would be attached to form, which is thus like a dream? Therefore, if the body does not [truly] exist, who is a [real] man and who a [real] woman?

Thus, it is inappropriate for an intelligent person to be attached to form, which is dream-like. The terms "man" and "woman" are designated on the basis of the differences between male and female bodies. Since the bodies that are the bases of those imputations are not found under analysis, how could a man or woman intrinsically exist?

Mindfulness of the feelings

88. If suffering exists in reality, why does it not prevent joyful experiences? If happiness [truly] exists, why do savory things and so on not brighten up the pain of grief and so on?

If the feelings[6] that we experience existed independently [i.e. truly existed], they would not depend on other circumstances. If that were the case, why would suffering not prevent joy? A person who experienced suffering could never feel happy. Moreover, if happiness were a self-defining entity, then on occasions of grief and so on, why would sensual sources of pleasure [e.g. food and drink] not bring one happiness?

89. You may say [such pleasure] is not experienced due to its being overridden by intense [suffering]. How then can something that is not experienced be a feeling?

Hypothesis: At times of grief there may be pleasure as well, but it is overridden by the more intense misery.
Response: Feeling is by definition of the nature of experience. So if something is not experienced, the term "feeling" cannot be applied to it.

90. You may maintain that there is subtle unhappiness [when there is great delight]; and while gross misery is removed, you may believe that [subtle discontent] is simply another pleasure. If that were the case, then even that subtle [satisfaction] would be [joy].

Hypothesis: When intense joy arises, even while there is subtle dissatisfaction, what feeling does that joy displace, such that it can be called "intense joy"? Does it not displace gross unhappiness? It removes gross misery, but subtle discontent remains. So that misery is not unexperienced; it is simply subtle. Moreover, that subtle dissatisfaction is actually a subtle form of pleasure, distinct from the intense joy.

Response: Since that subtle form of pleasure is a type of happiness, it cannot be classified as suffering. Even subtle pleasure is a form of happiness.

91. If you hold that suffering is not produced in the face
    of incompatible conditions, does this not imply that
    a "feeling" is a conceptual designation?

Hypothesis: When there is the experience of intense joy, which is incompatible with suffering, the latter is not produced.

Response: In this case you err in conceiving of feeling as being self-defining. The feelings of joy and sorrow do not exist from their own side. Although they exist as conceptual imputations, you cling to them as existing from their own side. Feelings do not exist by their own intrinsic nature; rather, they are identified on the basis of contributing circumstances.

92. Therefore, this analysis is cultivated as an antidote for
    that [false conception of intrinsic existence]. The
    meditative absorption that arises from the field of dis-
    criminative investigation is the food of the contem-
    plative.

Feelings do not truly exist; they are not found when sought through analysis; they do not exist independently, but exist by the power of convention. Thus, the means for overcoming the misconception of the true existence of feelings is meditation on their lack of such existence. This entails analyzing the mode of existence of feelings.

Such investigation is an aid to meditative absorption and leads to the integration of meditative quiescence and insight. That increases the physical vitality of the contemplative[7] and enhances the power of his [or her] spiritual practice. Thus it is called the nourishment of the contemplative.

93. If there is an interval of space between the sense organs and sensory objects, where is the contact between
the two? If there were no interval, they would become
one; in which case, what could contact what?

Now the author refutes the true existence of feelings. We
speak of feelings as being conditioned by contact with an object. An object is experienced by means of the combined in-
teraction of the object, the sensory organ and consciousness.
By that process feelings arise. So here the author analyzes contact to see whether it is truly existent or not.

If there were a spatial interval between the material particles that make up a sensory organ and those of the sensed object, where would the contact between them take place? If there
were no such interval between the elementary particles of the
sense organ and the object, they would indivisibly occupy the
same space. In that case they would become one. If particles
had exactly the same location, they would not be distinct, so
one could not speak of any contact between them.[8]

94. There is no interpenetration of two atoms, for there
is no empty space [in them] and they are of the same
size. If there is no penetration, no intermingling occurs; and if there is no intermingling, there is no contact between them.

One cannot speak of any interpenetration of atoms, since
atoms contain no empty space and are of the same dimensions.[9]
Moreover, if atoms do not penetrate one another, there could
be no intermingling of them, and thus there would be no contact among them.[10]

95. If they are partless, how is contact between them ever
supposed to be justified? If contact between partless
particles has been observed, please demonstrate it.

If at the subtlest level there is no space between atoms, they would be identical. If there *is* actual contact between atoms and if there is contact between them without their having any parts or attributes, this should be demonstrated.

96. Contact [by atoms] with immaterial consciousness is implausible; nor [is there contact among the atoms involved] in the conjunction [of sense organ and object], since they are not real, etc.

Here is an analysis of consciousness. The theory under inspection posits the production of cognition conditioned by (1) the sensed object as the objective condition,[11] (2) the sense organ as the dominant condition,[12] and (3) the preceding instant of consciousness as the immediate condition.[13] Since the third condition, consciousness, is immaterial, one cannot say that there is contact with it.[14] Moreover, there can be no true contact with a macroscopic collection of particles, for such a collection does not truly exist. This point was analyzed previously in the discussion of the parts of the body.[15]

97. Thus, if contact is not [truly] existent, how is feeling possible? What is the point of exertion? Who could be harmed by what?

For contact to take place, there must be the "contacter" and the "contacted." But if one seeks those imputed objects among the sensory object, sense organ and consciousness, no truly existent objects are found. Thus, contact does not intrinsically exist. Feeling arises in dependence upon contact, and if the cause does not truly exist, neither does the effect. So, whence could truly existent feelings arise?

Desiring to experience pleasant feelings and to avoid unpleasant feelings, people exert great effort towards those ends. But what is the point? What unpleasant feeling could harm what person? If one seeks the imputed object, one finds no harmful feeling nor any harmed owner of that feeling.

98. If any [truly existent] experiencer [of feeling] or [truly existent] feeling is not found, and one has recognized this situation, why do you not turn away from craving?

When a contemplative applies Centrist analysis in search of imputed objects, he [or she] discovers that no experienced object or experiencing self is to be found. In the face of such analysis, no feelings or experiencer of feelings exists. If one refrains from investigation and analysis, one can speak of an experiencer of feelings since one is endowed with feeling; and one can speak of feelings, since they are experienced. That is valid in a purely conventional sense.

But in a true, objective sense, if one were to speak of an experiencer who has feeling, one would be dealing with two entities: (1) the person who experiences and (2) apart from that, the experience itself. Then, as explained in Nagarjuna's *Fundamental Wisdom*, if the two are separate, there could be action without the agent of the action, and an agent unrelated to any action. That is impossible. Or [if one denies that they are separate, then] the action that enables us to speak of an agent would be identical with that agent. That, too, is a fallacy.

One discovers that no intrinsically existent feeling or experiencer is to be found. Now the mental affliction of craving arises due to mistakenly grasping onto the independent existence of objects. Thus, the confusion of grasping onto true existence is the basis of attachment and hostility. Once one has ascertained the non-existence of the object of such delusion, craving vanishes.

Subtle attachment and hostility are conjoined with the confusion of subtly grasping onto true existence. That conjunction is difficult to understand. For the most part, Buddhist philosophical systems from the Svatantrika on down claim that such cognition is objectively appropriate.[16] In fact, they seem to assert as appropriate the mere awareness of a pleasant object as being pleasant. So, while the Prasangika system regards as a mental affliction the subtle grasping onto true existence, which lies at the root of attachment and hostility, Buddhist

systems from the Svatantrika down to the Vaibhashika seem
to maintain that such grasping is appropriate.

Now gross attachment and hostility resulting from the mistaken sense of a self-sufficient, substantial personal identity
fundamentally arise from grasping onto true existence. If, using logical analysis, one refutes the object of such grasping,
such that grasping onto true existence does not arise, then the
mental distortions that are produced by that confusion are
averted.

As Chandrakirti states in his *Clear Words*,[17] that which acts
as an antidote to confusion acts as an antidote to all mental
distortions. On the contrary, specific antidotes to attachment,
anger and pride do not remedy all distortions. But the antidote to the confusion of grasping onto true existence acts as
a remedy for all mental afflictions.

99. That which is seen and that which is touched are of
    a dream-like and illusion-like nature. Because feeling
    arises together with the mind, it is not [ultimately] per-
    ceived.

There is nothing whatever that has a true mode of existence.
Nevertheless, this does not suggest that a person who experiences feelings and the feelings themselves—pleasant and
unpleasant—are utterly non-existent. They do exist, but in an
untrue fashion. Thus, the things that we see and touch have
a dream-like and illusion-like quality.

In the second line the author refutes the true existence of
the mind that experiences feelings. Since feelings arise in conjunction with the mind, feelings are not perceived by the mind
that is simultaneous with them. There must be a causal relationship between the experienced object and the experiencing subject. If two entities are substantially distinct and exist
simultaneously, there could be neither a causal relationship
nor an identity relationship[18] between them.

For this reason the author denies that either [intrinsic] relationship could hold for the feelings and the awareness that is

simultaneous with them. Two mental events that arise in conjunction with each other are not able to apprehend one another. This holds true for all states of awareness. Thus, feelings are not observed by the awareness that arises in conjunction with them and that exists simultaneously with them.

100. With two events arising sequentially, [the former] may
     be recalled but not experienced [by the latter]. Feel-
     ing does not experience its own nature, nor is it [truly]
     experienced by anything else.

A feeling is not observed by an awareness that exists prior to it, nor is it seen by a later cognition that exists after the feeling has ceased. It is incorrect to say that something observes itself, as this was established in the refutation of self-cognition. If one posits that one thing is experienced by something else [that is intrinsically different], this results in infinite regress.[19] Thus, in terms of true existence, experience cannot be posited at all.

101. There is not any [intrinsic] experiencer [of a feeling],
     and in reality there is no feeling. It being the case that
     this composite is identityless, who then is hurt by this
     [kind of unreal feeling]?

Since the experiencer of a feeling does not truly exist, feeling also does not exist in reality. So what harm can be inflicted upon this aggregate that is devoid of an identity or intrinsic nature?

While the psycho-physical aggregates of a person lack an intrinsic identity or self, we fail to recognize this and mistakenly become attached to those aggregates. But if we analytically seek the imputed object [the self], that fallacy is dispelled. How then could that [non-existent, intrinsic self] be harmed?

Grasping onto true existence is what makes us vulnerable to harm. Since there is no basis for such grasping, how can harm be inflicted [upon that non-existent basis]?

Mindfulness of the Mind

102. Mentality is not located among the sense organs, nor
     in form and so on, nor in between them. The mind
     is also not found inside [the person], nor outside, nor
     anywhere else.

Awareness is not located among the sense organs, nor among
the outer sensory objects such as visual form, nor in between
them. Some non-Buddhists believe that awareness exists in the
interior of a person, while others think that it exists in the
extremities of the body such as the hands.[20] But the mind does
not exist in either of those places, nor is it found elsewhere.

103. It is not [truly] in the body, nor somewhere else; it
     is not [truly] mixed [with the body] nor is it anywhere
     apart. It is not [truly] anything at all, so sentient be-
     ings are fully liberated.

The mind does not intrinsically exist in the nature of the
body, nor elsewhere, nor as a mixture with the body, nor on
its own apart from the body. If the imputed object, the mind,
is sought, one discovers that it does not exist independently.
Thus, sentient beings are by nature liberated.

The foregoing discussion concerns mental awareness. Now
the author goes on to analyze sensory awareness.

104. If awareness exists prior to the object of awareness,
     perceiving what, does it arise? If awareness is simul-
     taneous with the object of awareness, perceiving what,
     does it arise?

If sensory perceptions, such as visual awareness, exist prior
to their respective objects, in dependence upon what do they
arise? Visual awareness, for example, has to arise in dependence upon form as the objective condition for its occurrence.
So if visual awareness precedes its object, in dependence upon

what does it occur?[21]

If awareness and its object arise simultaneously, the same problem arises; for something that acts as the objective condition for the production of a cognition must precede that cognition. Causal relationships are necessarily sequential.[22]

105a.Moreover, were it to occur after its object, whence would awareness [truly] arise?

If awareness arises after its object has ceased, in dependence upon what would that awareness occur?

Mindfulness of Phenomena

105b.Thus, the [intrinsic] arising of all things is not ascertained.

Thus, when seeking the imputed object in terms of any entity whatever, one discovers that everything lacks independent existence. Everything exists in a relational way, purely by the power of convention.

Refutation of Objections

106. If that is so, conventional truth does not exist; so how could there be the two truths? On the other hand, because of another being's conventional truth, [conventional reality remains after one's own imaginative construction ceases]. If that is so, how is a being ever liberated?

Objection: You Centrists claim that no imputed object is found under analysis, and that emptiness itself does not exist. Upon seeking imputed objects, you conclude that there is no form, sound, smell, taste, tactile object nor mental object, and that there is no truth of suffering, truth of the source of suffering, truth of cessation or truth of the path. You say that everything does not exist.

You seem to maintain that all conventional realities that are involved in causal relationships are mere apparitions appearing to deluded minds, since they have no intrinsic existence. But if they are not intrinsically existent, they do not exist at all. In that case, how can there be the two truths? Ultimate truth would be out of the question, for it must be established on the basis of something that exists. But if that basis does not exist, it has no ultimate nature. Thus, relative and ultimate truth could not be posited.

If, according to you, everything that is posited consists purely of apparitions appearing to confused minds, then Nirvana would be impossible. Indeed, worldly judgements of "good" and "bad" would not hold up. Moreover, a cosmic primal substance, God, the Three Jewels of the Buddha, Dharma and Sangha[23] would all have the same status: If one of them exists, they all exist. For a confused mind such a primal substance may exist, God may exist, the horns of a rabbit may also exist. To a mind that conceives of rabbit horns, they exist. In short, if you say that something exists simply because it seems to be real to a deluded mind, nothing could be denied existence.

In that case "true" and "untrue," "good" and "evil," conventionally "existent" and "non-existent" all lose their meanings. One could no longer speak of false views, such as denying something which does exist and asserting something which does not exist. Thus, by undermining the distinction between "good" and "evil," there could be no liberation by means of correctly avoiding evil and adopting virtue. Moreover, liberation itself would be nothing more than an apparition of a deluded mind.

107. That construct [of one's liberation] in another's mind [would reify one's ultimate liberation; but it does not emerge] from one's own conventional reality. [And another's delusion cannot make something conventionally real, since] if something is [relatively] deter-

mined after [realizing emptiness], it [conventionally] exists; if not, it is not [even] a conventional reality.

The objection is that if something is said to exist merely because it is conceived by a deluded mind that grasps onto true existence, it would not be able to render help nor inflict harm. It would simply be an illusion.

Response: One cannot claim that something exists simply because it is conceived by a deluded mind.[24] So according to our [Centrist] system, that is not the criterion of conventional existence. When speaking of a "conventional truth," its truth is determined not by objective reality but by the mind. Objective reality cannot be the criterion for truth, for truth is of the mind.[25]

The [conventional] truths of the mind can be established only by the confusion[26] of grasping onto true existence. So when one speaks of "conventional truth," that is true for the mind that grasps onto true existence. However, the mind that establishes conventional reality must not be deluded.[27] It must be verifying.[28] It may be deluded with regard to its apparent object, but it must not be mistaken[29] with regard to its chief object.[30]

When establishing our own [Prasangika] conventional reality, a cosmic primal substance and God do not exist even conventionally. Likewise, in terms of other Buddhist views, we Centrists do not grant even conventional existence to the "foundation consciousness"[31] or "self-cognition" that are posited by the Idealist system. We regard things like jugs as conventionally existent. Both [entities and non-entities] are mere conceptual designations and neither exists from its own side. In that sense they are alike; but there is a distinction as to whether or not they are conventionally able to render help or inflict harm and whether or not they are established by a verifying cognition. That cognition is indeed deluded insofar as it is deluded with respect to the appearance of true existence. But apart from that, there is a distinction between being mistaken or unmistaken with respect to its chief object; and that is what determines whether it is a verifying cognition.

The criterion for conventional existence is the presence of a mind that is unmistaken with respect to its chief object. While ascertaining emptiness, one does not establish the existence of other entities. But upon rising from such meditative equipoise, if something appears clearly to the mind; if its conventional existence is not repudiated by any other conventional knowledge; if it is able to yield benefit or harm; and if it is established by verifying cognition—then it exists. If not, it does not exist even conventionally.[32]

108. The "conceptual mind" and the "conceived object" are mutually interdependent. All analysis is experienced in dependence upon, and in accordance with, common sense.

Subjective conceptual cognition and conceived objects are mutually interdependent. Action depends on an agent of action, and the agent depends on action. For example, a tailor is identified on the basis of his [of her] activity of tailoring; and since there are tailors, the activity of tailoring occurs. This is not to say that the agent and the action are causally related, but they are mutually dependent.

In order to establish the ultimate mode of existence of some entity, one must first determine that the entity in question exists. On that basis one inquires into its mode of existence.

109. Investigating the analysis of a subject of inquiry leads to infinite regress, for that analysis would also be subject to investigation.

Here is the question of infinite regress:
Objection: You Centrists first analyze some subject like a jug; then you investigate the ultimate nature of the jug. In this way you enter into an infinite regress of analysis.

110. Upon analyzing a subject of inquiry, [one sees that]

there is no [intrinsic] basis for that investigation. Since there is no basis, [that analyzing mind] does not [intrinsically] arise, and that is called [natural] "Nirvana."

Upon analyzing a subject such as a jug, one ascertains the intrinsic emptiness of the jug. That awareness apprehends the simple negation[33] that is the mere absence of the true existence of that subject. It cognizes only that emptiness. It apprehends no other entity; it does not identify "this" as opposed to "that." As long as that mode of cognition lasts, the subject, or basis, whose lack of true existence was investigated, is not ascertained by the mind.

Upon establishing the lack of intrinsic existence of entities of form and so on, if one further proceeds to analyze that ultimate reality[34] of the lack of intrinsic existence, one ascertains the lack of true existence of ultimate reality. In this case the subject of analysis is emptiness, and one ascertains the ultimate reality of the ultimate reality of forms and so on. Thus, one speaks of the emptiness of emptiness.

Part Three:
Refutation of True Existence

6 Refutation of Others' Conceptions of True Existence

111. According to some, both [awareness and its object]
    are truly existent; but that is completely untenable.
    If the object [truly] exists by the power of the aware-
    ness of it, what then is the justification for the [true]
    existence of awareness?

Realists assert that both awareness and its object are truly
existent; but that view is completely untenable. If the object
is truly existent on account of the true existence of awareness,
what grounds are there for maintaining the true existence of
awareness?[1]

112. Moreover, if awareness [truly] exists by the power of
    the object of awareness, what is the justification for
    the [true] existence of that object? Thus, as they ex-
    ist by the power of each other, neither would be [truly]
    existent.

Moreover, if awareness is established on account of a truly
existent object of awareness, what are the grounds for assert-

ing the latter? It is appropriate to posit their mutually dependent existence. But if one is not satisfied with that and insists
on an intrinsic basis for their existence, then inconsistencies
are inevitable.

Thus, if verifying cognition and its object exist in mutual
dependence—establishing each in relation to the other—neither
would be truly existent. They would both exist as mere con-
ventions in a relational sense; they would not exist by their
own intrinsic natures.

113. Without a father there can be no son, for where would
the son come from? But in the absence of a son there
is no father. Similarly, both [awareness and its object]
are not [truly] existent.

A father and child exist relative to one another. Without a
child, a father cannot be posited. It is strange: Until a child
is [physically] conceived, a man is not a father, for he cannot
be labelled as such. Thus, "father" is posited in relation to
a child, and before a child is conceived there is no father. Once
a child is conceived, there is a father. And yet one says that
a child is sired by its father. The man whose seed goes to help
produce a child is not a father prior to conception, but in reference to the child that will be produced later on, one can speak
of the father who sired the child. If one analytically seeks out
the father on his own, his existence cannot be posited. Thus,
the two are established relative to one another.[2]

114. Since a sprout arises from a seed, the [true existence
of] the seed is thereby revealed. Since awareness arises
from an object of knowledge, why is its [true] existence not ascertained?

Realist: One can infer the true existence of a seed by the
fact that it produces a sprout.[3] Likewise, why can one not realize
the true existence of an object of knowledge, since awareness
arises in dependence on it?[4]

115. The existence of a seed is understood because of a cognition that is different from the sprout. But whence comes an ascertainment of the [true] existence of awareness simply because an object of knowledge is apprehended?

Centrist: By ascertaining the causal relationship, one can know that a seed preceded a sprout. And one can know that an object of knowledge exists since it acts as a causal, objective condition for the arising of the resultant awareness of it. While apprehending an object of knowledge, by what verifying cognition is the awareness of that object ascertained?

7 Proofs of the Absence of True Existence

THE "DIAMOND-SPLINTERS" ARGUMENT

116. People do indeed perceptually observe all [kinds of] causes. The individual parts of a lotus, including its stalk and so on, are produced by various causal conditions.

Now the author establishes the lack of intrinsic existence of causes. First he makes a point of denying the absence of causality. For example, the individual parts of a lotus are produced by a variety of individual causes.

117. What makes the various causes?—a previous variety of causes. What makes a cause able to produce an effect?—the power of previous causes.

What accounts for the variety of causes? They too occur in reliance upon causal conditions. The ability of distinct causes to produce various distinct results is due to the power of each one's preceding cause.[1]

118. If you assert that Ishvara is the cause of living beings,
by all means let us know: Who [or what] is Ishvara?
You may reply: "the elements." That may be, but
then why even trouble yourself with a mere name?

As mentioned before, the qualities of our environment and
of sentient beings arise from causes, specifically by the power
of individuals' actions. The ability of good and bad causes to
produce good and bad results is due to the individual preceding conditions for those causes.

Objection: That is not right. Is there not a God who is the
cause of creation and destruction? Was the world not created
by Ishvara?[2]

Response: If you assert that God is the elements of Nature,
we agree with you. There is no fault in maintaining that living beings and the environment arise from the elements. But
there is no point in giving those elements the further name
of "God."

119. Furthermore, the earth element and so on are manifold, impermanent, inert and not divine; they are
stepped upon and are impure. That is not God.

Moreover, Ishvara is thought to be a unity, with absolute
power and immutable permanence. The earth element and so
on are many, impermanent, lacking a conscious ability to move
the elements, etc. and are not divine. They [e.g. earth and
water] are stepped upon and are impure. Thus, they cannot
be a sacred God.

120. Space is not the Mighty Lord, for it is inert; nor is
the self, for it has already been refuted. If the being
of the Creator is inconceivable, whatever is there to
say of that which is beyond thought?

Empty space cannot be regarded as God, the Creator, for
it is inert, being incapable of giving help or harm. Space is

divorced from any kind of action, and thus it is not God. A [permanent] self, or soul, is not God, for its existence has already been repudiated. It may be argued that God is inconceivable by ordinary people, but that is of no help.

121. What does Ishvara desire to create? The soul? Is not the nature of the soul, earth and so on, and the Lord immutable? Awareness is due to an object of awareness, without beginning.

What is it that Ishvara creates? The soul? Do you not maintain that the soul, the atoms that make up the four elements, and Ishvara are immutable? [If Ishvara is a Creator and the rest are creations,] this undermines your assertion of immutability.

According to our view,[3] sentient beings and our environment are produced by our own actions. Tracing the source of actions leads one to the mind. Thus, the source is awareness. This is not to say that the world is of the nature of consciousness. Actions are brought forth by wholesome and unwholesome states of awareness, and on this basis the world of phenomena is established.

Now awareness arises, taking on the image of its object, and it is the mere cognition of that object. Thus, conventionally speaking, awareness arises from its object. If one seeks that imputed object [awareness], it is not found. But without such analysis, one can posit consciousness simply in terms of appearances and conclude that it arises from its object.

Each specific state of awareness arises in dependence upon its own object, but fundamental consciousness is without beginning. From beginningless time it exists as simple awareness, or cognition, in an ongoing continuum.[4]

122. And joy and sorrow are due to action; so tell us: What is created [by Ishvara]? If the cause is without beginning, how could its effect have a beginning?

Specifically, joy and sorrow occur as a result of actions that are committed with wholesome and unwholesome states of mind. According to our view, the production, transformation and destruction of all natural phenomena can be understood without resort to the hypothesis of a Creator God.[5] Moreover, if you believe that God is an immutable, eternal cause having no beginning, how could there be a beginning to the effects of that cause?[6]

123. Why would they not always be produced, for Ishvara does not depend upon anything else? Since there is nothing that is not created by Him, upon what would He possibly depend?

Since Ishvara is believed to be immutable, if He produces something, it should be produced always. So why are all the effects of Ishvara not created simultaneously at all times? If there is nothing else that is not produced by Ishvara, He could not be influenced by any other conditions that might arise. He would be responsible for everything that occurs.

124. On the other hand, if [Creation] were dependent [upon conditions], the complete collection [of those causal circumstances] would be the cause, and not Ishvara. If the complete conditions were assembled, [Ishvara] would be powerless not to create; and if they were absent, there would be no creation.

If creation and destruction are dependent upon a collection of causal conditions, the totality of those conditions would be the cause, and not a God who is independent of and uninfluenced by events. If the causal conditions were assembled, Ishvara would be powerless not to create the resultant phenomena; and if they were not assembled, those phenomena would not be produced.

125. If Ishvara acts without desiring to, it would follow that

He is dominated by something else. Even if [He acts]
with the desire [to act], He would be dominated by
desire. In that case, what of [your concept of] divinity?

If, when causal conditions are assembled, Ishvara is forced
to create against His will, He would not be Lord of all Creation. Rather, He would be dominated by something else. Even
if His actions were preceded by willful intention, He would
not be independent and His actions would not be effortlessly
spontaneous. Rather, He would be dependent upon His desires.
Now desires are impermanent. They arise prior to action and
cease upon the completion of the desired action. Thus, the
belief in an immutable God is repudiated.

126. Moreover, those who claim that permanent atoms [are
the source of Creation] have already been refuted. The
Samkhyas assert a primal substance as the permanent
cause of the world.

Here is a reference to a Vaisheshika assertion, namely that
permanent atoms are the creators of the various worlds. This
was already refuted implicitly in the repudiation of partless
atoms.[7]

Next is a reference to a Samkhya view. A belief here is that
a single, permanent, cosmic primal substance, endowed with
five attributes, is the Creator. According to this view, all natural
phenomena included among the three types of perturbations
[of this substance] are subject to creation and destruction.

127. (They further) argue that the universal constituents
of "sattva," "rajas" and "tamas" in a state of equilibrium are the primal substance of the cosmos; and
the universe is said to be due to their disequilibrium.

When the three universal constituents of sattva, rajas and
tamas are in equilibrium, they are called "the primal substance," "absolute reality," or "the ultimate nature." If they

are in disequilibrium, perturbations occur [which manifest as the universe].

128. It is unreasonable that one [partless] entity should have three natures, so that [primal substance] does not exist. Likewise, the universal constituents are not [truly] found, for each one of those has three parts as well.

If the primal cosmic substance is posited as a partless unity, it is contradictory to maintain that it has the three natures of sattva, rajas and tamas. Thus, a primal substance that exists as an equilibrium state of the three universal constituents does not exist. It is inconsistent to claim on the one hand that it is a truly existent unity with no parts, and then on the other that its nature is the equilibrium state of three constituents.

Likewise, the theory of the three universal constituents does not hold up, for each of them is not a truly existent unity since each of them is a composite of all three constituents. Thus, one speaks of the "rajas element," the "tamas element," and the "sattva element" of the activity constituent and so on.[8]

129. And if the universal constituents do not [truly] exist, the [true] existence of sound and so forth is far-fetched. It is also impossible for there to exist joy and so on in mindless things such as cloth.

The theory of a primal substance and truly existent universal constituents is faulty. Thus, the corresponding assertion that sound and so forth arise from them as manifestations of them is utterly implausible.

Moreover, it is impossible that mindless material objects such as cloth and more generally the five sense objects[9] are substantially identical with joy, suffering and equanimity.

130. You may claim that things are of the nature of the causes [of happiness, etc.], but have things not already been analyzed? [You believe that the universal con-

stituents of] joy and so on are the causes, but such
things as woven cloth are not due to them.

Things such as cloth are not of the nature of joy and so on.
While you may say that the nature of the cause of cloth, etc.
is truly existent, that subject has already been analyzed.[10] According to your system, the cause of such things as cloth is
the primal substance, in which joy and so on are in equilibrium.
But woven cloth and so forth do not arise from that.

131. Even though pleasure, etc. may result from cloth, etc.,
when those [causes] are absent, pleasure is no more.
Thus, the permanence of pleasure, etc. is never ascertained.

You may say that such things as woven cloth give rise to
pleasure, etc. We refute the production of woven cloth, etc.
in terms of repudiating its basis of manifestation.[11] If you claim
that pleasure, etc. are due to such things as woven cloth, we
retort: Since woven cloth, etc. no longer exist, the resultant
pleasure, etc. no longer exist either. Thus, the permanence of
pleasure is never observed by means of verifying cognition.

132. If truly existent pleasure is observable, why is the experience of it not apprehended? If [you say that] it
becomes subtle, how can it be gross and [then] subtle?

If observable pleasure is a permanent, real entity, when
suffering is experienced, why is joy not experienced as well?
If joy is permanent, it should remain continually with no fluc-
tuations. If it becomes subtle at times of strong suffering, then
you must agree that it fluctuates from gross to subtle. But how
can it be subtle sometimes and gross at other times, since you
claim that it is immutably permanent?

133. It might be subtle after leaving its gross phase, but
then its grossness and subtlety would be imperma-

nent. Why then do you not accept all things as impermanent in the same way?

If there is fluctuation, such that it is subtle after being gross, it must be acknowledged that it is impermanent. Why then do you not assert that all things such as pleasure and so on are impermanent?

134. Its grossness is not something separate from pleasure, so the impermanence of pleasure is evident. You may believe that the unreal does not arise, for it has no existence whatever. Still, [the problem of] the creation of a non-existent manifestation remains for you, even against your will.

If its grossness is not substantially different from joy, joy is obviously impermanent, for it fluctuates from grossness to subtlety.

Next the author refutes the Samkhya belief in "self-creation."[12]

Samkyha: Any effect that is fundamentally non-existent at the time of its cause cannot arise. It must exist in order to arise. Thus, it cannot be utterly non-existent at the time of its cause; rather it exists potentially, but not manifestly. Then it arises into its manifest nature.[13] The manifest entity does not exist at the time of its cause, but its potentiality does exist.

135. If the effect is present in the cause, to eat food would be to eat excrement; and with the price of cloth one may as well buy cotton-seeds and wear them.

Centrist: If the substance of the effect is present in the cause, as you believe, then when one eats food one would be eating excrement; for the latter would be present in the former.

136. You may claim that worldly people do not see this

due to their confusion. But even for those who know reality that is the situation.

Samkhya: The effect is indeed present in the cause, but due to confusion, worldly people do not see this.

Centrist: Your teachers, such as the sage Kapila, who you believe directly know the nature of reality, would, according to you, realize that an effect is present at the time of its cause.

137. You maintain that knowledge of that exists in worldly people, too; so why do they not see it? If you counter that their cognition is not verifying, then their perception of manifest things is also unreal.

If the Samkhya belief that the effect is present in the cause is true, then worldly people should see this as well.[14] If worldly perception is not verifying, then such awareness of specific things in the world is not true.

138. If verifying cognition is not [ultimately] verifying, then indeed that which is known is deceptive. In reality the emptiness of phenomena is logically invalid.

Now the author responds to a criticism of the Centrist view:

Samkhya: Even according to your Centrist system, all states of awareness are deluded apart from a Superior's non-conceptual, meditative realization. So types of cognition that you call verifying are not ultimately verifying; even they are false. The verifying cognition that is the criterion for establishing the existence of entities exists only by the power of convention. It is not verifying due to any objective truth. Thus, objects that are known by that deluded "verifying" cognition must be false. In that case, the verifying cognition that identifies emptiness is false; and thus emptiness, too, must be deceptive. Then there is no point in meditating on emptiness.

139. Not having experienced any [true] thing as conceived,

its non-existence is not perceived [as a true thing either]. Therefore, when an existent thing is false, indeed, its non-existence is clearly false [as well].

Centrist: If the appearance of true existence, which is falsely imputed by ignorance, is not found, one does not apprehend its unreality. Thus, by repudiating this false entity, the deceptive nature of its unreality is clear. Even emptiness exists by the force of convention. If one analyzes it in relation to the object that is empty of an intrinsic nature, that emptiness is found to be devoid of true existence.

In short, every possible entity, without exception, lacks an intrinsic nature. If there were anything at all that was not empty of intrinsic existence, emptiness might be truly existent. But since everything is empty, it is impossible that emptiness is not itself empty.

Further, *Fundamental Wisdom* states that if one realizes the meaning of emptiness, this invalidates conceptual grasping to true existence; and attachment and hostility can thereby be dispelled. This acts as a remedy for suffering and discontent. However, conceiving of emptiness as being truly existent is said to be an incurable view. This is a very striking statement.

Thus, even emptiness exists simply by the force of convention. It does not truly exist. It does not exist in an ultimate sense. What is meant then when emptiness is said to be ultimate truth? The word "ultimate" is used in different ways. As explained in Maitreya's treatise *The Distinction between the Center and Extremes*,[15] there are ultimate objects, ultimate cognitions and ultimate proofs. The word "ultimate" may be applied to objects and subjects. When the two truths are explained in *Fundamental Wisdom*, the word "ultimate" refers to an object—emptiness. That is common in teachings of the Sutra tradition. In the Tantra tradition there are many instances when the same word is used in reference to the subjective mind. The "clear light"[16] state of awareness is frequently given the appellation "ultimate." Thus, one must be careful to recognize the context in which the word is used. Does it occur in explanations of the tantric stage of completion, or in the stage of development,[17] in the context of the lower classes of tantra, or in sutra contexts that bear no reference to tantra? If one fails to recognize such distinctions, one is liable to become confused.

Thus, there is much to be understood from the term as it is used in *The Distinction between the Center and Extremes.* Moreover, in the Svatantrika system there are references to a "simulated ultimate"[18] and an "ultimate." Even though emptiness is one entity, when it is experienced together with dualistic appearance, it is called a "simulated ultimate." When it is experienced without any dualistic appearance whatever, emptiness is called "ultimate." Although emptiness is a single entity, this distinction is made in terms of the way it appears to the mind. The word "ultimate" is also applied to the mind.

A further twofold distinction in the usage of this term is made: (1) All possible entities are deceptive and are not truly or ultimately existent. The true existence that is refuted in that statement is called "ultimate." Thus, emptiness, too, is deceptive and not ultimately existent. It exists by the force of convention, not by its own intrinsic reality. (2) Now emptiness is also called "ultimate truth." To the ultimate mind[19] that seeks the fundamental mode of existence of, say, a pot, its mode of existence appears. That mind does not find a pot, but the mode of existence of a pot. Since that mode of existence [i.e. the emptiness of an intrinsic nature of the pot] exists for that mind—since it is true for that mind—it is called "ultimate truth."

Thus, there is nothing whatever that is ultimate in the first sense, but in the second case the word "ultimate" is applied to something that does exist: a state of awareness that explores the fundamental mode of existence of entities. There are entities that are seen to exist by that mind, but they do not truly exist. If they were truly existent, they would exist by their own nature; and they should be apprehended by a mind that tries to determine whether or not they exist. If a pot were truly existent, it should be found by an ultimate mind that seeks the fundamental mode of existence of a pot.

The Buddha said that Nirvana is also emptiness. If there were something beyond Nirvana, it would be empty as well, in the sense that it would have no intrinsic nature. The finest entity—Nirvana—is emptiness. It was not newly created by the Buddha, nor by the minds of sentient beings. It has no intrinsic nature, but exists in a relative sense.

When we speak of emptiness, it may seem to be relatively impotent, for the entity that is empty [e.g. a pot] is more potent. We experience joy and sorrow due to the good and bad qualities of such entities; but there is no distinction of "good" and "bad" in terms of emptiness. It is strange: The mere absence of an intrinsic nature of an entity is emptiness, so emptiness seems sort of impotent. It depends upon that entity, so it does not exist on its own. It does not exist "apart from elaborations."[20] There are many kinds of elaborations: dualistic elaborations, elaborations of subjects, conventional elaborations and so on. Since emptiness does not exist apart from the elaboration of the subject that is empty, emptiness does not exist on its own. The simple negation that is emptiness exists by the negation of true existence, so of course it is deceptive [in the sense of not being absolute].[21]

140. Thus, upon the death of a son in a dream, the thought "he does not exist" obstructs the arising of the thought of his existence; and they are [both] deceptive.

Objection: What benefit is there in a deceptive, verifying cognition dispelling deceptive suffering?

Response: As it states in *Fundamental Wisdom*, everything is comprised of elaborations of elaborations, like deceptive illusions; but they are able to give benefit and inflict harm.

141. Therefore, such analysis reveals that there is nothing that is not due to a cause; and nothing is contained in either its single or combined causal conditions.

There is nothing that is produced without a cause, and nothing exists independently in either its individual or combined causal conditions.

142. An entity does not come from something else, it does not remain, nor does it depart. What is the difference between an illusion and that which is really fabricated by deluded people?

An effect is not present in any one of its causes nor in all of them together; it does not intrinsically remain upon having been produced; and upon its cessation, it does not go anywhere else.

The confusion of grasping onto true existence falsely imputes true existence upon entities; but whether that imputation is upon the causes, nature or effects of an entity, in fact they all exist only by the power of convention. However, things do not appear to exist merely by convention but rather from their own side. Thus, objects do not exist in the way they appear, and in that sense they are like illusions.

THE INTERDEPENDENCE ARGUMENT

143. You should deeply investigate whatever is created by an illusion and whatever is created by causes: Whence does it come and where does it go?

The point of this argument is that nothing is intrinsically created, abides or ceases. All phenomena are like illusions; they exist in a dependent fashion; and there is nothing that is independent.

144. One thing is seen by its juxtaposition with something else, but not if that other thing is missing. If something is artificially created, like a reflection, how can it be reality?

An effect is observed if it is in proximity to its causes, but if those causes do not exist, neither does the effect. Thus, it does not exist independently; its own existence is dependent upon something else. Since an effect depends upon its causal conditions, it does not exist on its own. Moreover, it exists in dependence upon its own components. There is nothing that exists on its own, independently of its parts or attributes; and upon analyzing the individual parts, no whole is to be found.

The basis of a designation and the object designated upon that basis are never identical, and the object is never found among the components of its basis of designation. Since the object does not exist from its own side, it exists simply by the power of conceptualization, or convention.

There is nothing that exists independently, by its own intrinsic identity, so everything is imputed, artificially created and reflection-like. How then can anything exist in reality? This is the "interdependence argument": Since things exist in reliance upon causal conditions, in dependence upon other things, how can they be truly existent, for they are like reflections?

THE ARGUMENT CONCERNING THE ARISING AND CESSATION OF ENTITIES AND NON-ENTITIES

145. If something truly exists, what does it need with a cause? Moreover, if something is non-existent, what does it need with a cause?

In general, existent things are produced, and non-existent things are not. However, in stating that entities are produced, if one means that they exist not simply by the power of convention, but by their own power, they would exist independently, without reliance upon other conditions. If something existed in that way, it would have no need for a cause, for it would already exist by its own power.

Moreover, if the phenomenon produced by its own power is non-existent—not non-existent merely due to an absence of contributing conditions—what good would causes do for it?

146. If something does not exist, there can be no change
in it, even by a million causes. How could its state
exist? What else could enter into a state of existence?

Even a million causes are not able to make something [in-
trinsically] non-existent become [intrinsically] existent. If the
state of non-existence is transformed into a state of existence,
it must do so either by shedding or not shedding its non-
existence. In the latter case, since existence and non-existence
are mutually exclusive, how could its state be existent? This
would be impossible. In the former case, apart from an existent and a non-existent, what else could become existent? There
is no other possibility.

147. If something does not exist when it is non-existent,
when does it become existent? And, by means of a
not [yet] produced existence, a non-existent [state] will
not be escaped.

When something is non-existent, it does not exist; so when
does it become existent? The author thus refutes the existence
of something that has not shed its non-existence. Moreover,
if something is not produced, it does not depart from non-
existence.

148. If something does not escape non-existence, it is impossible for its existence to emerge. And a [truly] existent entity cannot become non-existent, for it would
follow [absurdly] that it is of a dual nature.

Since the two states of existence and non-existence are mutually exclusive, if something does not depart from non-existence,
it cannot become an existent, nor can a [truly] existent entity
become non-existent. Why? Because it would follow that one
entity would have two mutually exclusive natures, and that

is impossible.

149. In that way, never is there any [true] cessation or [true]
     existence; and therefore this entire universe is un-
     produced and unceased.

Thus, there is no intrinsic cessation due to the vanishing
of causal conditions, nor is there any intrinsic reality that exists prior to cessation. Therefore, the entire universe, which
arises and passes simply by the power of convention, is devoid of intrinsic production, duration and cessation.

150. States of living are likes dreams, on analysis coreless
     like a plantain tree. In reality, there is no distinction
     between those who are and are not emancipated.

Like a dream, if one analyzes states of living, they are seen
to be devoid of an intrinsic essence, like a plantain tree.[22] Likewise, liberation and cyclic existence are devoid of an intrinsic
nature, and in terms of ultimate reality there is no distinction
between them.

8 *Encouragement to Strive to Realize Emptiness*

151. Thus, among empty phenomena, what could there
be to gain or lose? Who will be honored or despised
by whom?

In summary, an individual—e.g. oneself—who abides in the
cycle of existence, the dangers and suffering of this cycle, including mental distortions, and the attainment of Nirvana—
in short, all entities—are empty of an intrinsic nature. Thus,
what is to be attained, and what is to be lost? When one analyzes praise and blame, they are found to be not truly existent.

152. Whence come joy and sorrow, and what is pleasant
and unpleasant? When it is analytically sought in reality, what craving is there, and what does it crave?

In terms of friends and enemies, why should one be dis-
pleased with those who are unfriendly and why be pleased with
those who are friendly? If one seeks in terms of ultimate reality, who is it that craves, what is craved and what is the act
of craving? None of the three members of that triad intrinsi-

cally exist.[1]

153. Upon investigation, what is this world of living beings, and who really will die here? Who will there be,
and who was there? Who is a relative, and who is a
friend of whom?

154. Let those who are like me apprehend everything as
being like space. Due to the causes of strife, those
desiring their own happiness are provoked to anger,
and due to the causes of merriment they rejoice.

All phenomena are like space, and if they are investigated,
one finds that they are not self-sufficient but lack an intrinsic
identity. Initial understanding of emptiness will not immediately attenuate one's attachment and hostility; but by frequently
familiarizing oneself with that understanding, one gradually
approaches an actual realization of emptiness. In that process, dualistic appearance gradually fades away, culminating in
a direct, non-conceptual realization of ultimate reality. That
acts as a direct remedy for speculative mental distortions,[2] but
many other distortions are eliminated only upon the Path of
Meditation.

So it is difficult. Simply knowing the meaning of emptiness
does not suddenly free one from mental distortions. Rather,
by repeatedly ascertaining emptiness, distortions can gradually be dispelled.

155. [Driven by disturbing] troubles and disappointments,
they cut and stab one another and thus eke out an
existence in great hardship by means of evil deeds.

Next the author writes of the disadvantages of not realizing
emptiness. People who do not realize emptiness are enraged
by sources of conflict and delighted by sources of joy. When
their desires are not met, they experience misery; and to avoid
that they exert themselves, argue with one another, and cut

and stab each other. By such various evil deeds they make a living in great hardship.

156. Having repeatedly entered fortunate states of existence and experienced delightful joys, the dead fall to miserable destinations in which there is protracted, violent anguish.

Even in this life, due to attachment and hostility, there is little joy but great hardship. In the hereafter most people wander in miserable states of existence. Even when in a fortunate state of existence, they do not investigate the root of the cycle of existence or meditate on emptiness; and as a result they descend again to miserable destinations. There they experience protracted, violent suffering.

157. There are many abysses in the world, and no such [understanding of] reality is to be found there. [Ignorance and understanding of reality] are mutually incompatible, and in cyclic existence there is no such [understanding of] reality.

There are many abodes of suffering, and in the many abysses of the cycle of existence there is ignorance of the nature of reality. Thus, one is bound to this cycle by the fetters of craving.

Grasping onto true existence is incompatible with experiencing the nature of reality, and thus in this cycle of existence people do not ascertain reality.

158. And there are boundless oceans of incomparable, violent suffering. Thus, there is feebleness and short lifespan as well.

In this cycle of existence manifold types of suffering and discontent are to be experienced, and one has little ability to engage in wholesome activity.

159. There, too, [they seek] long life and health by means of their occupations, with hunger, exhaustion, weariness, sleep and calamities, and with meaningless association with childish people.

160. Thus, life passes by swiftly and in vain, with very little opportunity for discrimination [between good and bad]. Where is there a way to prevent habitual distraction?

161. There, too, Mara tries to cause beings to fall to deeply wretched states; and due to a multitude of false paths, doubt is difficult to overcome.

People let their time pass in distractions, and the wisdom of investigating the nature of phenomena is exceedingly rare. Even if there is some modest inclination toward spirituality, due to habituation with distraction, it does not tend to be sustained, nor go very deep. It is difficult to remedy that habituation.

Furthermore, much harm is wrought by Mara[3] and other such entities, which obstruct people's spiritual practice. In this world there are a great many false paths that lead to suffering. For instance, there are extreme views such as nihilism; and there is agnosticism, which is difficult to transcend.

162. It is difficult to obtain leisure[4] again, and the presence of a Buddha is extremely hard to find. It is difficult to restrain the flood of mental distortions. Alas, suffering continues uninterruptedly!

163. Alas for those in intense grief, for those adrift in a flood of suffering, for those in terrible situations who, nonetheless, fail to recognize their own miserable state!

While abiding in limitless suffering, people do not recognize their own state of existence, their own discontent. Rather, they mistake suffering for happiness. They are worthy of our sympathy.

164. Some people repeatedly perform ritual ablutions followed by entering fire. Although they dwell in a state of misery, they think they are in a fine condition.

165. For those who pretend that there is no aging or death terrible calamities are encountered and they are slain by them.

Those who pretend to be carefree, acting as if they were Liberated Beings who had overcome aging and death, are first slain by impermanence, then fall to miserable destinations.

166. With the rain of my joy that springs forth from the clouds of virtue, when might I be able to soothe those who are tormented by the fires of misery?

167. By having gathered the store of merit and by not seizing upon conventional truths, when might I manifestly demonstrate emptiness to those who have fastened on false views?

May I realize the basis, path and fruition of spiritual practice without grasping onto true existence, but recognizing their mere conventional existence. May I accumulate virtue with a motivation of compassion. With a unification of my practice of wisdom [viz. realization of emptiness] and my practice of virtue, motivated by compassion for sentient beings, may I become fully awakened. May I reveal emptiness to those limitless sentient beings who are afflicted by grasping unquestioningly onto true existence. Thus, a Bodhisattva prays that any ability resulting from meditation on emptiness may be used only to bring about the welfare of others.

Notes

Foreword

[1]Sanskrit: *Bodhisattvacāryāvatāra*.

[2]Madhyamika philosophy traces back to the Buddha's own teachings. This philosophical view was first systematized by the Indian sage Nagarjuna several centuries after the Buddha's death. Thus, Shantideva, living in the eighth century of the Christian era, was dealing with a philosophical system that had already been studied and practiced for over a millennium in the rich intellectual and spiritual environment of classical India.

[3]Tibetan: *sPyod 'jug shes rab le'u'i tikka blo gsal ba*. The chapter titles and other headings within Book II are based chiefly on Tsongkhapa's outline in the above commentary.

[4]Sanskrit: *Pañjikā*.

[5]*sPyod 'jug rnam bshad rgyal sras 'jug ngogs* by rGyal tshab dar ma rin chen.

[6]I attended that series of discourses and have here translated the commentary to Shantideva's ninth chapter from recordings.

The Place of Wisdom in Spiritual Practice

[1]The first five transcendent practices are generosity, moral discipline, patience, enthusiasm and meditative absorption. The sixth is transcendent wisdom.

[2]Skt.: dhyāna, Tib.: bsam gtan. Throughout the text, when two terms are cited in a footnote, the first, as in this case, will be in Sanskrit and the second in Tibetan. If only one term is cited, it will be in Tibetan.

[3]śrāvaka, nyan thos.

[4]pratyekabuddha, rang rgyal.

[5]For a concise explanation of the Listeners and Solitary Sages see H.H. the Dalai Lama's *Opening the Eye of New Awareness* (Wisdom Pub., London, 1985) pp. 85-90. Listeners, Solitary Sages and Bodhisattvas attain their respective degrees of spiritual awakening by developing along their five respective paths. These are the: (1) Path of Accumulation, (2) Path of Preparation, (3) Path of Seeing, (4) Path of Meditation and (5) Path of No Training. A person suited for the Listener's Vehicle, for example, attains the Listener's Path of Accumulation upon achieving effortless, pure renunciation. The Path of Preparation is reached upon completing the Path of Accumulation and experiencing integrated meditative quiescence and insight into the nature of emptiness. Such realization is mixed with the general idea of emptiness. The Path of Seeing is reached upon gaining direct realization of emptiness free of the veil of even the most subtle conceptualization. The Path of Meditation entails repeated insight into ultimate truth, thereby dispelling all mental distortions. The Listener's Path

of No Training is reached when that process of mental purification is complete: The mind is now completely free of mental distortions together with the "seeds" for their arisal. The Five Paths of Solitary Sages and Bodhisattvas differ from those of Listeners, and they culminate in higher degrees of awakening. For further explanation of those three sets of the Five Paths see Geshey Ngawang Dhargyey's *Tibetan Tradition of Mental Development* (Library of Tibetan Works and Archives, Dharmsala, India, 1974) pp. 183-201.

[6]kleśāvaraṇa, nyon mongs pa'i sgrib pa. These obscurations include primarily confusion, craving and hostility.

[7]śamatha, zhi gnas.

[8]vipaśyanā, lhag mthong.

[9]jñeyāvarana, shes bya'i sgrib pa. These include, for example, the instincts of mental afflictions and the appearance of things as being truly existent.

[10]For an explanation of meditative quiescence and insight based on the scriptures of Theravada Buddhism, see Amadeo Sole-Leris's *Tranquility and Insight* (Shambhala Publications, Boston, 1986) and Henepola Gunaratana's *The Path of Serenity and Insight* (South Asia Books, Columbia, Missouri, 1985). A Centrist explanation of these two facets of Buddhist practice is given in Jeffrey Hopkins' *Meditation on Emptiness* (Wisdom Publications, London, 1983) pp. 67-110.

[11]By engaging in wholesome activities of the body, speech and mind one accumulates a "store of virtue." Such behavior places beneficial imprints upon the mind, and these are an indispensable aid to spiritual awakening. Buddhist practice continually emphasizes the balance between the cultivation of wisdom and involvement in altruistic activity motivated by compassion. Further reference to the two types of obscurations is given in *Medi-*

tation on Emptiness, p. 300.

[12]abhyudaya, mngon mtho. This refers to birth in the fortunate realms of existence as a human being, a demigod or a god.

[13]nihśreyasa, nges legs.

[14]bodhicitta, byang chub sems. This spirit of awakening entails the aspiration to achieve the full spiritual awakening of a Buddha in order to be of benefit to all sentient beings. Further explanation can be found in Jeffrey Hopkins' *The Tantric Distinction* (Wisdom Publications, London, 1984) pp. 58-74.

[15]For an explanation of the Buddhist concept of cyclic existence see *Meditative States in Tibetan Buddhism* by Lati Rinbochay, Denma Lochö Rinbochay, Leah Zahler and Jeffrey Hopkins (Wisdom Publications, London, 1983) pp. 23-47. Liberation from this cyclic existence is called "Nirvana."

[16]The Three Trainings are in moral discipline, concentration and wisdom. See *Opening the Eye of New Awareness,* pp. 53-84.

[17]kleśa, nyon mongs. I have translated this important term both as mental distortion and mental affliction, so they are used synonymously. The first translation brings out the fact that *klesas* distort our experience of reality and thereby lead us into suffering. The second translation emphasizes that they are maladies of the mind, suggesting both that they are a source of pain and that the afflicted mind can be healed.

Introduction to the Two Truths That Comprise Reality

[1]Throughout this text the term "phenomenon" will be used synonymously with "entity," rather than as an antonym to "noumenon."

²The cycle of existence is the condition of being repeatedly subject to birth, aging, sickness and death due to the power of mental afflictions and the actions that are tainted by them.

³vāsanā, bag chags.

⁴pratītyasamutpāda, rten cing 'brel bar 'byung ba.

⁵The Sanskrit term *dharma* is translated in this work in three ways—entity, phenomenon and event—so those terms should be regarded as synonymous.

⁶ji lta ba'i shes rab. This is contrasted with "phenomenological understanding" (ji snyed pa'i shes rab), which concerns the manifold events of conventional reality.

⁷In this translation the term "Idealist" is used only with reference to the Buddhist idealist school known as Vijñānavāda (Tib. *sems tsam pa*).

⁸The term "Centrist" here refers only to the Madhyamika school (Tib. *dbu ma pa*) of Buddhist philosophy.

⁹don spyi.

¹⁰The same analogy may also be interpreted in different ways by contemplatives having different levels of insight. For example, both Idealists as well as Centrists assert that the physical world is dream-like. Idealists interpret this as meaning that while the world appears to the senses as if it exists externally, independent of the mind, in fact all phenomena are of the nature of consciousness. The Prasangikas, in contrast, assert phenomena as dream-like on the grounds that they appear to be truly existent, whereas they are actually devoid of inherent existence. Both interpretations accept the dream analogy due to the lack of accord between the way phenomena appear and the way they exist.

[11]If one applies ultimate analysis to the recipient of one's generosity, no person is to be found. This same negative result occurs if such investigation is applied to the giver and the act of giving. This conclusion, however, should not prevent one from acts of generosity. When engaging in such service, one regards the giver, the act of giving and the recipient in terms of conventional reality, without applying ultimate analysis to them.

[12]According to the Prasangika view, to posit the existence of something, three criteria must be fulfilled: (1) Its existence must be accepted in terms of conventional cognition, (2) It must not be invalidated by conventional cognition and (3) It must also not be invalidated by the type of cognition that investigates ultimate truth. Note that all three criteria concern cognition; none touch on any determining factor from the side of the object. This view is scripturally based upon the Buddha's statement: "Those things that the public asserts as existent, I too assert as existent. Those things that the public deems non-existent, I too deem non-existent."

[13]pramāṇa, tshad ma. For an explanation of the two major types of verifying cognition, perceptual and inferential, see F. Th. Stcherbatsky's *Buddhist Logic* (Dover Publications, New York, 1962) Vol. I, pp. 146-180, 231-274.

[14]rang mtshan.

[15]An entity does not exist by its own intrinsic being, but in dependence upon conceptual designation. In this sense it exists by the power of consensus; but, as the author points out, the mere fact that a certain group of people believe in the existence of something does not necessarily mean that it exists. For example, during the nineteenth century, there was widespread belief among physicists in the existence of absolute space and time. Although there was, roughly speaking, a consensus, that belief was erroneous.

A cognition may be mistaken with respect to the appearance of its object while not mistaken with respect to the object itself. For further reference to this point see the footnote 25 to verse 75.

[16]An "impure object" commonly cited in Buddhist literature is the human body. Sexual attraction toward the human body entails viewing it as something "pure" and desirable, and this appearance is enhanced by the use of perfume, jewelry and attractive garments. When the mind is dominated by lust, one focuses on the exterior of the desired body and associates it with desirable qualities. The contemplative whose mind is free of sensual craving sees that the body is "impure" as this term is normally used; for the outer skin is a container for such substances as blood, fat, bone, phlegm, sweat, excrement and urine. The deluded mind of a lustful person ignores the presence of these impure components of the body and falsely regards it as pure.

[17]To sum up, a community of people may agree as to the existence of certain entities and their ultimate mode of existence and yet be wrong. The fallacy of such beliefs is due to the fact that they are invalidated by verifying cognition; it is not because they fail to correspond to some independent, absolute reality. A central challenge of Buddhist mental training is to recognize the difference between deceptive and verifying cognition and to cultivate the latter. This is the purpose of the threefold training in moral discipline, concentration and wisdom.

[18]"Tainted things" include those things that arise under the influence of mental distortions and the actions that ensue from such distortions.

[19]The Four Noble Truths, together with their sixteen attributes, are discussed in *Tibetan Tradition of Mental Development*, pp. 20-38.

[20]To the untrained mind, the phenomena around us seem fairly static; only their gross impermanence is seen. The awareness of a contemplative, on the other hand, is refined to the point that the very subtle, moment-by-moment arising and passing of phenomena is ascertained. This subtle impermanence is an important facet of conventional reality.

[21]The mind of a contemplative is refined by means of a formidable training in stabilizing and clarifying awareness through the practice of meditative quiescence. It is then further developed with methods for the cultivation of insight. In this way verifiable knowledge is gained concerning both conventional and ultimate reality, and this invalidates the unfounded assumptions of common people.

[22]Thus, the Centrist theory states very plainly that truth is not established by "majority rule." The insights of the enlightened few may invalidate the consensus of the masses. When Shantideva first orally presented this treatise, he did so before a congregation of monks; so it was appropriate for him to refer to the impurity of the female body as an antidote to lust. Were such a teacher to speak before an assembly of nuns, the reference would quite possibly be to the impurity of the male body.

[23]In committing a deed, four processes occur: (1) the intention, (2) the preparation, (3) the enactment and (4) the culmination of the act. In "killing" a mindless illusion of a person, the first two of those stages may occur, but not the latter two. Clearly the actual deed of killing and the resultant death of one's victim cannot occur, for no person exists in the illusion. Thus, the evil of slaying another person does not occur, but there is still the evil of the intent and the preparation.

[24]This subject is discussed in the commentary to verse 96. According to Buddhist contemplative science, the mind does not originate from matter or energy, nor does it arise from noth-

ing. Rather, it can arise only in dependence upon a preceding mental continuum. Thus, the initial moment of consciousness of a fetus does not originate from the union of the egg and sperm of its parents. It must arise from a preceding continuum of consciousness. This continuum can be traced back to a previous life in which it was conjoined with another body that lived and died. The mind of a fetus thus carries innumerable imprints from previous lives.

25 *Yuktiṣaṣṭikā, Rigs pa drug bcu pa.*

26Further reference to residual and non-residual liberation can be found in *Meditation on Emptiness*, pp. 342, 394-395.

27A Buddha has gained release from the cycle of existence, but this does not imply, according to Mahayana Buddhism, that such a being no longer takes birth in the world. He [or she] does not take birth due to the force of mental distortions and the actions that are tainted by them. Rather, a Buddha appears in the world due to the force of compassion, in order to lead sentient beings to spiritual awakening.

28The Buddhist concept of the world as illusion is one that is commonly misunderstood by Western readers. This is partially due to a large body of Buddhist literature in Western languages that misrepresents this theory. This distortion of the Buddhist teachings naturally creates unjustified barriers between the Buddhist and the Western scientific search for truth.

For example, when physicist Stephen Hawking was presented with the possibility that Eastern mysticism might yield insights into objective reality, he responded, "I think it is absolute rubbish . . . The universe of Eastern mysticism is an illusion. A physicist who attempts to link it with his own work has abandoned physics." [*Stephen Hawking's Universe*, John Boslough (William Morrow & Co., New York, 1985) p. 127]. The mere fact that Buddhism deems the world to be illusion-like hardly sets it at odds with Western science. The transcendental realism underlying most of even classical physics states that nature is drastically unlike our direct experience of it; and both quantum mechanics and relativity describe a world very foreign to our ordinary perceptions and concepts. In that sense science deems everyday experience of nature as illusory. The very existence of the objective world has also been challenged on the basis of recent research in quantum mechanics (cf. "Is the moon there when nobody looks?: Reality and quantum theory," N. David Mermin, *Physics Today*, Apr., 1985, p. 38; "The Quantum Theory and Reality," Bernard d Espagnat, *Scientific American*, Vol. 241, No. 5, Nov. 1979).

The Centrist view acknowledges the existence of a physical world every bit as real as mental events, and it states that physical theories may be true of nature insofar as they are based on verifying experience. In this way it avoids the extreme of instrumentalism. However, science does not represent nature as it exists independently of our experience and concepts; and with this statement the Centrist view shuns the extremes of both immanent realism and transcendental realism.

[29]dharmadhātu, chos kyi dbyings.

Critique of the Idealist View

[1]dhātu, khams. The three are the sensual realm, the form realm and the formless realm.

[2]*Cūḍāmaniṣūtra, bTsug na rin po che'i mdo.*

[3]*Prajñāmūla, rTsa ba'i shes rab.*

[4]gzhi grub.

[5]btags don.

[6]svasaṃvitti, rang rig.

[7]For a method to develop such awareness see Buddhaghosa's *The Path of Purification*, trans. Bhikkhu Ñāṇamoli (Buddhist Publishing Society, Kandy, Sri Lanka, 1979) XIII, 8-12.

[8]For an explanation of this practice see Geshé Rabten's *Echoes of Voidness* (Wisdom Publications, London, 1983), pp. 113-128.

[9]The possibility of such an alchemically produced ointment seems to have been common knowledge during the time of Shantideva, and contemporary traditional Tibetan Buddhists also accept this discussion literally.

[10]Here is one of innumerable references in Buddhism to the close relationship between morality and inquiry into the nature of reality. Ignorance in the form of actively misapprehending reality is regarded as the fundamental distortion of the mind, and it is the source of other afflictions such as craving and hostility. Such mental distortions move people to evil behavior, and this is the source of strife and misery. Thus, the Buddhist quest for truth is not unrelated to ethics, as is so much of Western science and philosophy.

[11]gnas lugs su grub pa.

[12]bāhyārtha, phyi don.

[13]rnam pa.

[14]btags yod.

[15]abhāva, dngos med.

The Necessity of the Centrist Path

[1]āryamārga, 'phags lam.

[2]samādhi, ting nge 'dzin.

[3]cf. note 5 to verse 1.

[4]vajropamasamādhi, rdo rje lta bu'i ting nge 'dzin.

[5]Impure realms of existence are those that come into being by the power of mental distortions and the actions that ensue from such distortions. According to Buddhist cosmology, the world in which a community of sentient beings dwells is brought into existence by the former deeds of the members of that community. No transcendent creator is needed for the creation of worlds. A pure realm is one that is brought about by the prayers of an Awakened Being, and it is untainted by mental distortions and the actions that ensue from such distortions.

[6]Shantideva makes reference to such strange phenomena as "medicinal pillars" as if their existence was commonly accepted by his contemporary audience. The classical Indian civilization of his time abounded in "psychic technology" due to its advanced contemplative science. In the intervening centuries such knowledge has declined in part due to the impact of Western civilization upon traditional Indian culture.

[7]The realist looks upon the causal relations between natural events as a compelling reason for believing that they exist in their own right, independent of conceptual designation. If they were dependent upon such designation, how could they ever interact among themselves? The Centrist replies that if events were truly existent, they would be utterly immutable and isolated from one another. Each entity would intrinsically bear its own static attributes, and it would exist eternally. This would

preclude any possibility of causal interactions among phenomena. In short, the Centrist concludes that causal relations are possible only because events are not truly existent.

[8]There are different ways of interpreting identitylessness and emptiness as they appear among the sixteen attributes of the Four Noble Truths. One interpretation regards identitylessness as the absence of a self-sufficient, substantial I, and emptiness as the absence of a self-sufficient, substantial "my" and "mine." A grosser interpretation identifies these terms with the absence of "I," "me" and "mine" in terms of an unchanging, independent, unitary personal identity. Both interpretations fall short of the depth of the Centrist view of emptiness.

[9]These four stages are (1) Stream-Enterer, (2) Once-Returner, (3) Non-Returner and (4) Arhat (Liberated Being). For an explanation of these stages according to Theravada Buddhism see Paravahera Vajirañāṇa Mahāthera's *Buddhist Meditation in Theory and Practice* (Buddhist Missionary Society, Jalan Berhala, Kuala Lumpur, Malaysia, 1975), ch. 30.

[10]For an explanation of the difference between Hinayana and Mahayana see *The Tantric Distinction*, pp. 93-102.

[11]tīrthika, mu stegs pa

[12]*Ratnāvalī, dBu ma rin chen phreng ba*

[13]*Sūtrālaṃkāra, mDo sde rgyan*

[14]cf. Buddhaghosa's *The Path of Purification*, trans. Bhikkhu Ñāṇamoli (Buddhist Publication Society, Kandy, Sri Lanka, 1979) XXII 33-43.

[15]cf. *ibid.*, III 128, IV 55, XIII 16.

[16]These three baskets are (1) Vinaya, dealing with moral dis-

cipline; (2) Sutra, dealing with the training in meditative concentration and other facets of the path of awakening; and (3) Abhidharma (sometimes translated as "higher knowledge"), concerning a diversity of topics ranging from psychology to cosmology. For a further explanation see *Opening the Eye of New Awareness*, pp. 47-52.

[17]las dag.

[18]For a brief introduction to the meaning of tantra in the Buddhist context see *Opening the Eye of New Awareness*, pp. 95-105.

[19]zab gsal gnyis med.

[20]cakravartirājā, 'khor los bsgyur ba'i rgyal po. This refers to certain righteous kings discussed in Buddhist scriptures who variously reign over one, two, three or all four sectors of the earth.

[21]These are explained in *Death, Intermediate State and Rebirth*, Lati Rinbochay and Jeffrey Hopkins (Snow Lion Publications, Ithaca, New York, 1985). See also Geshe Kelsang Gyatso's *Clear Light of Bliss* (Wisdom Publications, London, 1982) pp. 17-32.

[22]For an introduction to Vaibhashika philosophy see Th. Stcherbatsky's *The Central Conception of Buddhism* (Motilal Banarsidass, Delhi, India, 1974) pp. 76-91.

[24]asaṃjñisamāpatti, 'du shes med pa'i snyoms 'jug.

[24]None of the verses 49-51 appear in the Sanskrit version edited by P.L. Vaidya (Buddhist Sanskrit Text Series), though they are present in other Sanskrit editions and Tibetan translations.

Personal Identitylessness

¹pudgalanairātmya, gang zag gi bdag med.

²dharmanairātmya, chos kyi bdag med.

³The Sanskrit *ātman*, (Tib. *bdag*) is here usually translated as "identity," whereas in other Buddhist translations it is often rendered as "self." The Centrist view refutes the existence of two types of *ātman*, that of persons and that of other entities. The Centrist thus speaks of the lack of an *ātman* of a table, for instance. In English it is appropriate to speak of analytically seeking the identity of a table, but the notion of a self of a table is peculiar. We may indeed speak of a "table itself," but in reference to a table, we would not normally speak of "its self." Thus, I have usually chosen to use the broader term "identity." The exceptions, as in the above case, occur when the *ātman* in question *is* of a personal nature.

⁴This is similarly true in the investigation of other entities. First one must clearly ascertain the phenomenal nature of the entity in question, and thereafter one can proceed to investigate its ultimate mode of existence.

⁵btags gzhi.

⁶The six are the five types of sensory consciousness and mental consciousness.

⁷btags don.

⁸For a helpful table setting forth these terms in a systematic way see Robert A.F. Thurman's translation of Tsong Khapa's *Essence of True Eloquence* (Princeton University Press, Princeton, NJ, 1984) p. 139.

⁹The Samkhya system asserts that there are an infinite num-

ber of selves. The nature of the self is existence and conscious-
ness. It is without parts, and it experiences pleasure and pain.
For an extensive introduction to Samkhya philosophy see *A
History of Indian Philosophy* by S. Dasgupta (Cambridge
University Press, Cambridge, 1922) Vol. I, Ch. VII.

[10]vikāra, rnam 'gyur.

[11]svabhāva, rang bzhin.

[12]snying stobs.

[13]rdul.

[14]mun pa.

[15]For an explanation of these three constituents see S. Dasgupta's *A History of Indian Philosophy*, Vol. I, pp. 243-247.
Dasgupta translates *sattva*, *rajas* and *tamas* respectively as
"intelligence-stuff," "energy-stuff" and "mass-stuff." He comments (p. 245) that "in the phenomenal product whatever
energy there is is due to the element of rajas and rajas alone;
all matter, resistance, stability, is due to tamas, and all conscious manifestation to sattva."

[16]guṇa, yon tan.

[17]prakṛti, gtso bo. When the Samkhyas speak of a pervasive
primal substance whose perturbations result in the manifold
world of natural phenomena, we may be reminded of specu-
lations in modern physics concerning the role of the vacuum
in the cosmos. Some physicists believe that the entire universe
originated from a fluctuation of the energy of the vacuum.
However, there are significant differences between the two
views. Astronomer E. R. Harrison claims that the original state
of the universe was one of irrational, indeterministic chaos.
On the other hand, P. T. Raju writes [*The Philosophical Tra-*

ditions of India, (George Allen & Unwin Ltd., London, 1971) p. 161.] that the primal substance of Samkhya cosmology "is not a chaotic stuff, but something in which everything is in harmony and equilibrium. We cannot attribute order to it, because the concept of order implies plurality among the members of which definite, fixed relations exist. Prakrti is originally absolute equilibrium, but completely undifferentiated."

[18]svabhāva, rang bzhin. This term is often translated as "nature." However, when used in the context of *ekasvabhāva*, the translation "substantially identical" seems most fitting; hence the present translation.

[19]cf. *A History of Indian Philosophy*, Vol. I, pp. 245-248.

[20]While the Samkhya philosophy asserts the existence of a plurality of selves, it fundamentally treats the material world as a unity, namely the primal substance. This unity appears in a plurality of forms, and even time and space have no separate existence. It appears in the same way for every self, and it is independent of any self. Although it is not sentient, mind is one of its products; thus, it is the original stuff of the psychophysical world. On the relationship between the self and the primal substance P. T. Raju comments: "The original distinction, for the Samkhya, is not between mind and matter, but between the *ātman*, which is infinite consciousness, but indeterminate and Prakrti, which is the infinite unconscious, but determinate. It is out of this infinite, but determinate unconscious that the manifold world evolves." (*The Philosophical Traditions of India*, pp. 160-161).

[21]astitā, yod pa nyid.

[22]For an extensive introduction to the Nyaya-Vaisheshika philosophy see S. Dasgupta's *A History of Indian Philosophy*, Vol. I, Ch. VIII.

²³This concept of the self is common to most non-Buddhist Indian philosophies.

²⁴Like a point on a line, it disappears when precisely sought.

²⁵'khrul pa'i tshad ma. A verifying cognition must be unmistaken with respect to its chief object (*'jug yul*), viz. the main object that it ascertains. However, it may at the same time be a deceptive cognition with respect to its appearing object (*snang yul*). For example, a verifying inferential cognition correctly ascertains the inferred object. But since that object and the *idea* of that object appear to such cognition as if they were fused together, this cognition is deceptive with respect to that appearance. Why? Because that object and the idea of it do not exist in the manner in which they so appear. According to the Centrist view, a perceptual verifying cognition can also be deceptive with respect to its appearing object. That object appears to be truly·existent, but in fact it is not.

²⁶In this verse the Sanskrit *ahaṃkāra* (grasping onto the ''I'') reads in the Tibetan translation as *nga rgyal*.

Phenomenal Identitylessness

¹smṛtyupasthāna, dran pa nye bar gzhag pa.

²The Tibetan reads ''hand'' and ''fingers,'' whereas the present version of the Sanskrit reads ''foot'' and ''toes or fingers'' (*aṃguli* means either, depending on the context). The Tibetan version seems to be a slightly more likely reading.

³aṇu, rdul.

⁴Further reference to Buddhist views concerning atoms is found in S. Anacker's *Seven Works of Vasubandhu* (Motilal Banarsidass, Delhi, India, 1984) pp. 167-170. This passage entails

an Idealist refutation of the existence of atoms.

[5]This form of analysis of the ontological status of the atom pertains both to the classical and quantum mechanical concepts of the atom and subatomic particles. The atom or particle may or may not be conceived as having a definite size and location, but all theories attribute to it certain defining characteristics. Otherwise, it would be wholly indistinguishable from other entities. As soon as the particle is conceived as bearing certain qualities, we may proceed with the analysis: What is the relationship between the whole and its parts? The conclusion is that particles of matter are as devoid of intrinsic existence as is space.

[6]The term "feeling" (*vedanā, tshor ba*) as it is used here has a more limited meaning than is usual in English. It refers to physical and mental feelings of pleasure, pain and indifference. It does not include, for instance, the tactile sensation that arises when one touches an object.

[7]yogin, rnal 'byor pa.

[8]Recall that in modern quantum field theory the concept of individual elementary particles remains very problematic. Moreover, there is considerable disagreement among contemporary physicists concerning the actual nature of atoms. Physicist d'Espagnat claims that they are mere properties of space; Stapp argues that they are a set of relationships; and Heisenberg denies that they are things. The Centrist theory does not deny the existence of atoms; but it does refute the assumption that they exist as real entities independent of conceptual designation.

[9]This statement would be contested by most contemporary physicists, citing the work of Rutherford in 1911, who experimentally demonstrated that most of the interior of an atom is composed of empty space. This idea is closely related to the

"planetary model" of the atom, in which the electrons orbit about the nucleus. Now modern quantum theory, with its wave/particle duality and uncertainty principle, states that this model cannot be regarded as a representation of the atom as an objective reality. The model is useful (and in broad use) as a heuristic device. Furthermore, according to modern quantum field theory, "empty space" seems to be far from empty. However, in the context of this Buddhist text, it is more important to recognize that the Buddhist concept of atoms differs radically from that of modern Western science. Buddhist contemplatives have used their own heightened powers of awareness, developed through rigorous training in meditation, as their means of exploring the smallest components of the physical world. Modern physicists use mechanical instruments and mathematics in formulating their atomic theories. In this situation much insight can be gleaned from Heisenberg's comment: "What we observe is not nature in itself but nature exposed to our method of questioning." Given these two radically different methods of questioning, it is hardly surprising that the resultant theories differ as much as they do.

Given the major differences between Buddhist contemplative views concerning the basic constituents of the natural world and the views of modern physical science, we may ask: which is more useful? But this question needs to be refined: useful for what purpose? In terms of advancing technology, the theories and models of physics and chemistry are incomparably more useful; but in terms of transforming one's body and mind through contemplative practice, the views of Buddhist contemplatives are far more appropriate.

[10]Once again, this statement must be understood within the context of Buddhist atomic theory. It would be inappropriate to equate the Buddhist usage of the term "atom" with that of modern physics. Having emphasized this point, it may be of interest to note that modern physics is far from certain as to the manner in which particles of matter do interact. Are they interconnected by a system of fields, or is Schwinger's

"source theory," which dispenses with fields, truer of physical reality? The Einstein-Podolsky-Rosen Paradox and Bell's Theorem also pertain to such questions.

[11]ālambanapratyaya, dmigs rkyen.

[12]adhipatipratyaya, bdag rkyen.

[13]samanantarapratyaya, de ma thag rkyen. See *The Mind and its Functions* by Geshé Rabten, trans. by Stephen Batchelor (Tharpa Choeling, 1801 Mt. Pelerin, Switzerland).

[14]Buddhism does clearly make a distinction between mind and matter, or between cognitive and physical events. Cognitive events, such as sensory awareness, memory and imagination, *experience* their respective objects. Physical entities, acting as objective conditions and dominant conditions, may certainly contribute to the production of various forms of cognition; but they themselves experience nothing. Although there is abundant evidence for believing that certain neurophysiological processes are necessary for normal visual perception to occur, what scientific grounds are there for equating the two? Materialists may suppose that perception is nothing more than a physical process, but who has ever experientially verified this theory? Now the Centrist view acknowledges the role of the three types of conditions mentioned in the commentary, but it denies that any such interactions have real, intrinsic existence. Moreover, the causal interactions between physical and cognitive events go both ways: Subjectively experienced cognitive processes affect physical processes, as do physical influence the cognitive.

[15]cf. verse 85.

[16]don mthun.

[17]*Prasannapadā, Tshig gsal.*

[18]bdag gcig 'brel. An identity relationship is present when distinct entities exist simultaneously and are of the same nature. For example, the red color of an apple bears an identity relationship with the apple.

[19]cf. verse 22.

[20]There is a common belief nowadays that visual perceptions, thoughts, and mental images are located in the brain. That the brain is involved in the arising of these cognitive events is undeniable and is hardly a recent discovery. But where is the evidence that these subjectively experienced events occur in the head or anywhere in physical space? For a critique of this assumption by a Western philosopher, see E. A. Burtt's *The Metaphysical Foundations of Modern Physical Science*, Chapter 8 (b).

[21]This verse makes it quite clear that the Centrist view avoids not only the extreme of materialism but of idealism as well. Physical phenomena do indeed depend for their existence upon mental designation, but perceptions of the physical world, such as visual cognition, require for their production objective conditions. The Centrist view does acknowledge a dualism between cognitive and physical events, but the two are seen as mutually interdependent. Moreover, the dualism itself has purely a conventional status; it, too, exists in dependence upon conceptual imputation.

[22]Although causal relationships are sequential, cause and effect are not separated by absolute, objective time. According to the Centrist view, not only are effects dependent upon their causes, but causes depend upon their effects.

[23]For an explanation of the Three Jewels see *Tibetan Tradition of Mental Development*, pp. 60-69.

[24]Here the fallacy of extreme relativism is avoided. Although

entities exist in dependence upon conceptual designation, it is not true that one person's concepts are necessarily as valid as another's; nor is it true that each person lives in his or her own reality determined solely by that individual's beliefs. For example, one who is convinced that death entails complete personal annihilation is not extinguished at death simply because of that mistaken view. We may deny things that do exists; and though we are influenced by such false views, we do not escape influence by the things that we deny. Similarly, we may believe in things that do not exist. We are then influenced by such false beliefs, but not by the non-entities that we believe in. The central purpose of Buddhist mental training is to recognize and discard those two types of false views. This is done by means of cultivating verifying perceptual and inferential cognition.

[25]Although this statement seems as first glance to suggest idealism, a subtler meaning is intended. According to the Centrist view, truth cannot be determined on the basis of some reality existing independently of the mind; for such a reality does not exist. However, this is *not* to say that there is no reality existing independently of the *human* mind. Precisely stated, the human mind can neither perceive nor conceive a reality independent of itself. Truth is determined on the basis of its knowability by a verifying cognition. A truth may not be known by a given individual or society, but this does not mean that it does not exist. If something is apprehended by *any* verifying cognition, it exists.

[26]moha, gti mug.

[27]abhrānta, ma 'khrul ba. The Buddhist terminology in this section is very precise, and it is difficult to avoid confusion in the English translation. The mind that establishes conventional reality must not be *deluded* in terms of mistakenly apprehending its chief object. For example, a mind that believes in rabbit's horns is deluded with respect to its chief object,

viz. rabbit's horns. A mind that establishes conventional reality is termed *confusion* only because it grasps onto true existence. It correctly identifies its chief object, but it mistakenly regards that object as truly existent.

[28]According to the Centrist view, a cognition is verifying if it unmistakenly apprehends it chief object.

[29]avisaṃvādaka, mi slu ba.

[30]'jug yul. For anyone but a Buddha, a fully awakened being, all conventional truths appear as if they were truly existent. Thus, when an ordinary person sees a mountain, it falsely appears to exist intrinsically from its own side. One may unmistakenly apprehend the mountain (the chief object), while being deluded with respect to its mode of appearance (the apparent object).

[31]ālayavijñāna, kun gzhi rnam par shes pa.

[32]It has already been mentioned that there are generally two kinds of verifying cognition: perceptual and inferential. The former includes valid sensory cognitions as well as certain kinds of mental awareness in which objects are ascertained without the appearance of the *ideas* of those objects. Inferential verifying cognition apprehends its object in dependence upon conclusive reasoning; and such cognition is always mixed with the appearance of the idea of its object. Because of the twofold nature of verifying cognition, Tibetan Buddhist mental discipline entails training both in meditation and logic. The former is aimed primarily at cultivating subtle forms of perceptual, mental verifying cognition. With such training one can eventually ascertain for oneself the existence of such events as past and future lives. A central emphasis of this discipline is to learn to distinguish between verifying cognition and the fantasizing mind that conjures up all sorts of fictitious imagery.

[33]med dgag.

[34]dharmatā, chos nyid.

Refutation of Others' Conceptions of True Existence

[1]Here, once again, the Centrist view takes a stand essentially different from that of idealism.

[2]The mutual dependence between father and child is obvious in terms of language. And because, conventionally speaking, there can be no father without a child or child without a father, this is true of the reality that is imputed by convention. The same is true of the mutual dependence between cause and effect: One cannot speak of a cause without an effect or vice versa. Thus the two are interdependent in terms of language and conventional reality.

[3]This is the Realists' major rationale for asserting the true existence of natural phenomena: They are causally interrelated, so they must exist independently of conceptual designation. The Centrist replies: It is precisely because such interrelationships occur that it is impossible for those phenomena to be self-defining, intrinsic entities.

[4]Here is another major Realist argument: The world about us must truly exist, otherwise we would not share common experience of it, which arises in dependence upon that independent, objective world. Indeed, until one has deeply explored the role of consciousness in the universe, the above conclusion seems inescapable. Western science has hardly begun to make such an exploration, so it naturally assumes the true, independent nature of the cosmos. Buddhist contemplative science has long engaged in such empirical investigation into the nature and function of consciousness; and it accounts for shared, common experience in terms the role of shared actions in previous lives and their effects in this life.

Note that the Centrist view acknowledges the role of objective conditions for the occurrence of perceptions of the natural world. But it denies that those conditions exist *independently* of mental imputation.

Proofs of the Absence of True Existence

[1]Buddhism very clearly asserts the importance of causality in the occurrence of both physical and cognitive natural events. Recall that mind is considered to be as much a constituent of the universe as matter or space; and causal relationships pertain equally in cognitive and physical events as well as to the interactions between those two types of phenomena. Prevailing interpretations of quantum mechanics emphasize the lack of strict causality in the quantum world. This view, which first became popular in Western Europe during the era between the two World Wars, prefers the themes of chaos, randomness and uncertainty governing the basic constituents of the natural world. This historical context does lead one to ponder the extent to which this ontological view was influenced by the social and economic climate of the times. In any case, it is a fallacy to equate the Buddhist view of causality with either the mechanistic determinism of classical physics, or the probabilistic determinism of quantum physics.

[2]As implied by the context, "Ishvara" is regarded in Hinduism as the personal Creator of the universe.

[3]cf. verse 117.

[4]According the Buddhism, no new continuums of consciousness are ever created. The mental continuum of every sentient being traces back to beginningless time. A wide variety of life forms are taken on by each consciousness in diverse physical realms of existence. A sentient being may even dwell in formless realms which are unaffected by the cycles of cosmic origi-

nation and destruction. Moreover, while one cosmos is undergoing total destruction, making it unfit for any type of corporeal life forms, others are being born, while yet others are abiding in a habitable state. Buddhist cosmology asserts the existence of countless worlds inhabited by countless sentient beings including humans, animals and a myriad of other life forms. Even our own planet is the home of many non-human, non-animal sentient beings. Although normally hidden from human senses, they can be apprehended upon refining one's consciousness by means of certain types of meditation.

[5]In his paper entitled "Science and Religion" Albert Einstein declares: "The main source of the present-day conflicts between the spheres of religion and science lies in this concept of a personal God" [*Out of My Later Years*, Albert Einstein (Philosophical Library, N.Y., 1950) p. 27]. Buddhism denies the existence of a Creator God, as it attributes the creation of the world to natural events rather than to a source beyond nature. It is essential to keep in mind, however, that by "natural events" Buddhism includes many phenomena, including consciousness, which Western science normally excludes from the natural world.

[6]The notion that the universe and all the sentient beings who dwell in it have no ultimate beginning is often hard to grasp by the Western mind. Although the distortions and obscurations of an individual stream of consciousness have no beginning, they are irrevocably dispelled upon full awakening. The conscious continuum of a Buddha then continues on to a endless future; and the limitless activities of a Buddha focus entirely on leading others to spiritual awakening. Western thinkers are often accustomed to thinking in terms of ultimate beginnings, and both in the spheres of religion and science they are admonished not to ask what happened prior to such beginnings. Buddhism denies any beginning to time, and it refutes the existence of a Creator existing outside of time on the grounds that there is no verifying cognition of either.

[7]cf. verses 93-95.

[8]A contemporary explanation of them can be found in I.K. Tainmi's *The Science of Yoga* (The Theosophical Publishing House, Wheaton, Ill., 1981), pp. 171-179. For a more traditional account see Swami Hariharananda Aranya's *Yoga Philosophy of Patañjali* (State University of New York Press, Albany, N.Y., 1981), pp. 158-169.

[9]tanmātra, de tsam. See *Yoga Philosophy of Patañjali*, pp. 169-170.

[10]cf. verses 78-87.

[11]'khrul gzhi.

[12]ātmaja, bdag skyes. The Samkhya system, finding it difficult to accept that non-being can become being, asserts that the effect, even before it occurs, was being. However, the effect is only latently present in the cause, and its production makes manifest what is already latent. Thus, causation is only a manifestation of what is already potentially existing. On a cosmic scale, the world is produced from the primal substance, but this is simply a manifestation of what that substance already contains. This subject is discussed in S. Dasgupta's *A History of Indian Philosophy* (pp. 254-258) and P.T. Raju's *The Philosophical Traditions of India* (pp. 162-163). In his book *Physics and Philosophy: The Revolution in Modern Science* (Harper & Row, Pub., N.Y., 1962) Werner Heisenberg discusses his own belief in a "Universal substance" (p. 61) and his theory that unmeasured atoms and particles exist as "potentia" (p. 186), which are not as real as the phenomena of daily life.

[13]Recall that Heisenberg regards unmeasured entities in the quantum world as existing as potentialities which, by the act of measurement, enter the actual realm of manifest reality. A

parallel may be drawn between that view and the present Samkhya theory. The Centrist view refutes both insofar as they posit such potentialities as truly existent.

[14]If this is perception of realized beings, and worldly people will eventually become realized, then that resultant realization should already be present in them. Thus, they should see that effects are present in their causes, just as the sages of the Samkhya school do.

[15]*Madhyāntavibhaṃgakārikā, dBus mtha' rnam 'byed.*

[16]cf. *Clear Light of Bliss*, pp. 203-213.

[17]For an explanation of these two stages see Daniel Cozort's *Highest Yoga Tantra* (Snow Lion Publications, Ithaca, N.Y. 1986) pp. 39-114.

[18]mthun pa'i don dam.

[19]This mind is called "ultimate" because it is involved in ultimate analysis of an entity, seeking its essential mode of existence.

[20]niṣprapañca, spros pa dang bral ba.

[21]Buddhist philosophy speaks of two types of negations: simple (*med dgag*) and complex (*ma yin dgag*). The former is the mere absence of something. Non-composite space, for example, is defined as the mere absence of obstruction, and it is, thus, a simple negation. A complex negation consists of the absence of something, together with the affirmation of something else. Thus, a treeless plain is a complex negation: Trees are negated, while the plain is affirmed.

[22]From the outside, a plantain tree seems firm and solid, but if one penetrates it, one discovers that it has no core. Its appearance belies its reality.

Encouragement to Strive to Realize Emptiness

[1]The triad of agent, action and object of the action is a frequent subject of analysis in the Centrist system. If we relate this to scientific research, we can speak of the person who makes a measurement, the system of measurement and the measured object. All three are mutually interdependent, and none bears an intrinsic identity. If the person in this triad reifies his or her own individual existence, there will be a tendency to reify the act of measurement and the measured object as well. From the Centrist perspective, this guarantees that such research will be conducted under a cloud of ontological confusion.

[2]Speculative mental distortions are those that one acquires by adopting false views and so on. They have to be *learned*. Inborn mental distortions are those that one is born with. Thus, a newborn infant enters the world with mental obscurations carried over from previous lives; and these may then be compounded with speculative distortions that are adopted during its lifetime. Buddhist practice is aimed not at reverting to an infant-like state of consciousness, but at striving toward an unprecedented state of awakening. Inborn mental distortions are finally dispelled only as one develops on the Path of Meditation.

[3]The "devil" for Buddhists. The term "Mara" is used sometimes in the singular and sometimes in the plural.

[4]In Buddhist literature "obtaining leisure" refers to meeting with outer and inner conditions that are crucial for fully effective spiritual practice. Eighteen factors of "leisure" and "endowment" are frequently discussed in this regard. See H.H. the Dalai Lama's *Path to Enlightenment*, translated and edited by Glenn H. Mullin (Snow Lion Publications, Ithaca, N.Y., 1994; formerly titled *Essence of Refined Gold*) pp. 58-62.

Bibliography

Anacker, S. *Seven Works of Vasubandhu.* Delhi: Motilal Banarsidass, 1984.

Aranya, S.H. *Yoga Philosophy of Patañjali.* Albany: State University of New York Press, 1981.

Buddhaghosa, B. *The Path of Purification.* Translated by B. Ñāṇamoli. Kandy, Sri Lanka: Buddhist Publication Society, 1979.

Burtt, E.A. *Metaphysical Foundations of Modern Physical Science.* New York: Harcourt, Brace, & Co., 1927.

Dalai Lama, H.H. *Opening the Eye of New Awareness.* London: Wisdom Publications, 1985.

Dalai Lama, H.H. *Path to Enlightenment.* Translated by Glenn H. Mullin. Ithaca, New York: Snow Lion Publications, 1994. Formerly entitled *Essence of Refined Gold.*

Dasgupta, Surendranath. *A History of Indian Philosophy.* Cambridge: Cambridge University Press, 1922.

Dhargyey, Geshe Ngawang. *Tibetan Tradition of Mental Development.* Dharamsala, India: Library of Tibetan Works & Archives, 1974.

Gyatso, Geshe Kelsang. *Clear Light of Bliss.* London: Wisdom Publications, 1982.

Hopkins, Jeffrey. *Meditation on Emptiness*. London: Wisdom Publications, 1983.

Hopkins, Jeffrey. *The Tantric Distinction*. London: Wisdom Publictions, 1984.

Mahāthera, P. Vajirañāna. *Buddhist Meditation in Theory and Practice*. Kuala Lumpur: Buddhist Missionary Society, 1975.

Rabten, Geshe. *Echoes of Voidness*. Translated by Stephen Batchelor. London: Wisdom Publications, 1983.

Rabten, Geshe. *The Mind and its Functions*. Translated by Stephen Batchelor. Mt. Pelerin, Switzerland: Tharpa Choeling, 1980.

Raju, P.T., *The Philosophical Traditions of India*. London: George Allen & Unwin, Ltd., 1971.

Rinbochay, Lati and Jeffrey Hopkins. *Death, Intermediate State and Rebirth*. Ithaca, New York: Snow Lion Publications, 1985.

Rinbochay, Lati, et. al. *Meditative States in Tibetan Buddhism*. London: Wisdom Publications, 1983.

Solé-Leris, A. *Tranquility and Insight*. Boston: Shambhala Publications, 1986.

Stcherbatsky, Theodore. *Buddhist Logic*. New York: Dover Publications, 1962.

Stcherbatsky, Theodore. *The Central Conception of Buddhism*. Delhi: Motilal Banarsidass, 1974.

Tsong Khapa. *Essence of True Eloquence*. Translated by Robert A. F. Thurman. Princeton: Princeton University Press, 1984.